The Philosophy of
Open Learning

GLOBAL STUDIES IN EDUCATION

A.C. (Tina) Besley, Michael A. Peters,
Cameron McCarthy, Fazal Rizvi
General Editors

Vol. 32

The Global Studies in Education series is part of the Peter Lang Education list.
Every volume is peer reviewed and meets
the highest quality standards for content and production.

PETER LANG
New York • Bern • Frankfurt • Berlin
Brussels • Vienna • Oxford • Warsaw

The Philosophy of Open Learning

Peer Learning and the Intellectual Commons

Edited by Markus Deimann
and Michael A. Peters

PETER LANG
New York • Bern • Frankfurt • Berlin
Brussels • Vienna • Oxford • Warsaw

Library of Congress Cataloging-in-Publication Data
Names: Deimann, Markus, editor. | Peters, Michael (Michael A.), editor.
Title: The philosophy of open learning: peer learning and the intellectual commons /
edited by Markus Deimann, Michael A. Peters.
Description: New York: Peter Lang, 2016.
Series: Global studies in education; vol. 32 | ISSN 2153-330X
Includes bibliographical references.
Identifiers: LCCN 2015048222 | ISBN 978-1-4331-2858-5 (hardcover: alk. paper)
ISBN 978-1-4331-2857-8 (paperback: alk. paper) | ISBN 978-1-4539-1821-0 (ebook pdf)
ISBN 978-1-4331-3604-7 (epub) | ISBN 978-1-4331-3605-4 (mobi)
Subjects: LCSH: Open learning—Philosophy.
Classification: LCC LC5800.P53 2015 | DDC 378/.03—dc23
LC record available at http://lccn.loc.gov/2015048222

Bibliographic information published by **Die Deutsche Nationalbibliothek**.
Die Deutsche Nationalbibliothek lists this publication in the "Deutsche
Nationalbibliografie"; detailed bibliographic data are available
on the Internet at http://dnb.d-nb.de/.

The paper in this book meets the guidelines for permanence and durability
of the Committee on Production Guidelines for Book Longevity
of the Council of Library Resources.

© 2016 Peter Lang Publishing, Inc., New York
29 Broadway, 18th floor, New York, NY 10006
www.peterlang.com

All rights reserved.
Reprint or reproduction, even partially, in all forms such as microfilm,
xerography, microfiche, microcard, and offset strictly prohibited.

Printed in the United States of America

Table of Contents

Foreword vii
    Martin Weller

Introduction: Open Education—The Past, the Present and the Future. 1
    Markus Deimann and Michael A. Peters

Chapter One: Constellations of Openness 11
    Robert Farrow

Chapter Two: Openness and the Intellectual Commons 23
    Michael A. Peters

Chapter Three: Opening Up Education: Opportunities, Obstacles and
    Future Perspectives. 31
    Petra Missomelius and Theo Hug

Chapter Four: MOOCs, Neoliberalism and the Role of the University 51
    David Small

Chapter Five: Posthuman Openings: Looking Beyond
    Technology Instrumentalism 67
    Jeremy Knox

Chapter Six: Of Two Contrasting Philosophies That Underpin Openness
   in Education and What That Entails 83
   Peter B. Sloep and Robert Schuwer

Chapter Seven: Another World Is Possible: The Relationship Between
   Open Higher Education and Mass Intellectuality 101
   Richard Hall

Chapter Eight: Open Access, Freedom and Exclusion 117
   Martin Oliver

Chapter Nine: Open Learning and Social Innovation: Freedom and
   Democratic Culture 129
   Michael A. Peters, Richard Heraud and Andrew Gibbons

Editors 147

Foreword

MARTIN WELLER

The 'open' of 'open education' has become a much more ambiguous term over the past decade or so. Although the roots of open education go back much further, the modern interpretation of open education has largely been aligned with the development of open, distance education models, such as that pioneered by The Open University in the United Kingdom. More recently, the influence of open source software, open approaches from the Web 2.0 sphere, open access publishing, open education resources (OER) and massive open online courses (MOOCs) has seen a wider interpretation of what openness means in education. There has been a rise in the popularity of both the term and its uptake by mainstream education.

However, this burgeoning popularity of all things open has led to confusion around the term itself. Does it apply to traditional distance education or openly licensed content or free courses? There is a danger in the term becoming essentially meaningless. Allied to this is a sense that much of the work in the open education field is implementation driven, for example, the development of open textbooks to supplant expensive, proprietary ones.

The field, however, in its more recent, broader interpretation, is reaching a state of maturity. Creative Commons was founded in 2001 and MIT launched its OpenCourseWare project in 2002. While the early phases of a field are often typified by application and advocacy as it reaches a level of maturity, more reflective, critical analysis is both possible and essential.

The work in this edition is a significant component of this emerging critical approach applied to open education. What does openness in education mean? What are its theoretical foundations? What implications does it have for new forms of education? These are the types of questions this book seeks to address. As we see more people appropriating the 'open' label because it has market value, establishing a theoretical basis for openness will be increasingly important. To be able to reference work such as this and come to a common understanding of the philosophy of open education will enable it to emerge as a discipline in itself. The focus thus far has largely been on the application of open approaches within disciplines, but there is a sense that open education can also be viewed as a multi-disciplinary field in its own right.

This edition is a timely and critical contribution to this emerging field. The political aspects of open education are explored in a manner that is largely absent from most publications in this field, including neoliberalism and Marxism. Combined with philosophical underpinnings and the relation to humanism and the Enlightenment, the edition provides a firm grounding for the views that often shape open education but are rarely made explicit.

Introduction: Open Education—The Past, THE Present AND THE Future

MARKUS DEIMANN AND MICHAEL A. PETERS

There has been much interest in open education over the last decade, which can be interpreted as another sign of the ongoing transformation from an industrialized to a knowledge-based digital society. Open education has been resurrected as a reform project with a long tradition in education history, going back at least to the Enlightenment, which brought about ideas of free speech and communication (e.g., via free press). With the advancement of innovative information and communication technologies embraced under the label "Web 2.0," social production of knowledge (e.g., Wikipedia), open standards and licenses and a new way of receiving and distributing information have emerged with profound impact on educational practices. Openness seems to articulate an attitude that resembles the core spirit of education, which centers around the notion of sharing. On a deep cultural level, this involves the moral obligation of parents to raise awareness of the various meanings of sharing in the process of enculturation. It is also expected that teachers—as well as experienced individuals in general—share their knowledge to ensure the prosperity of a society. Interactions and collaboration are based on the willingness of sharing—not only information and time but also "soft things," such as feelings of discovery and joy.

The liberal story of education and education as an engine of modernity is a history of increasing openness, politically linking education to the open society and its norms of freedom and equality. One dominant expression was succinctly stated by Immanuel Kant in "What is Enlightenment?" as "Dare to think for yourself!"

where thinking is equated with "public reason" and its expression. Yet this history also highlights the troubled story of the relation between education considered as a fundamental human right and the constitutional right to freedom of speech. Philosophically, it might be argued that open education is a technological embodiment and affordance of the link between these rights. Freedom of speech as a right is traditionally justified in terms of the promotion of the free flow of ideas essential to political democracy and its institutions, especially as embodied in the institution of a "free press." Ultimately, free speech limits the ability of the State to subvert other rights and freedoms. Perhaps most importantly, free speech is said to depend on the search for truth and thus is related to education insofar as it rests on the latest science. Educational theorists are also quick to point out how free speech is a significant personal and psychological good that promotes self-expression and thereby autonomy, the development of the self together with self-representation, identity and cultural belonging.

These justifications firmly relate questions of the self and self-governance to questions of democratic government, the search of truth and personal autonomy; while they suggest that there are overriding reasons for accepting that free speech is a basic political principle, they also imply free speech is not an absolute concept but a limited notion because it always takes place within a context of competing values (Mill, 2002). The modern discussion of free speech from John Milton and John Stuart Mill has drawn attention to limiting conditions expressed as principles, such as Mill's principle of harm or Joel Feinberg's principle of offense, especially where it can be demonstrated that so limiting free speech prevents damage to other rights. Freedom of speech in liberal society therefore exists in a tight network of rights and constraints that limit it. Momigliano (1973/2003) commented as follows:

> The modern notion of freedom of speech is assumed to include the right of speech in the governing bodies and the right to petition them, the right to relate and publish debates of these bodies, freedom of public meeting, freedom of correspondence, of teaching, of worship, of publishing newspapers and books. Correspondingly, abuse of freedom of speech includes libel, slander, obscenity, blasphemy, sedition (pp. 252)

While openness in general both in political and educational terms defines and gives shape to the open society, the question is how it will shape an emerging global society and to what extent these freedoms and limitations can be developed and understood in a digital context.

We need to be cautious lest open education and education in a digital world simply become machines for producing digital labor (Peters & Bulut, 2011). The classic defense of the liberal society as the open society cannot ignore questions of political economy. Karl Popper's normative logic for open scientific inquiry was also postulated as a model for political philosophy and theory where he criticized Plato, Hegel and Marx for advancing a utopian society based on the allegedly inexorable historicist logic of modernity. Yet he provided only a set of principles that operate at a metalevel rather than a substantive social philosophy, and he did not work out the implications of a commitment to the open society at the level of everyday communication (Moldoveanu, 2000). *The Open Society and Its Enemies* (Popper, 1945) was written as his "war effort," Popper tells us at the beginning of the Cold War, well before the transition to the networked media society where information and communication technologies have fundamentally changed all aspects of our daily lives and redefined cultural production and consumption. He was not able to see how systems of meaning are becoming digital or the ways in which digital information can be infinitely copied, globally shared and distributed and endlessly transformed. Opderbeck (2007) said the following:

> "Open" intellectual property rights (IPR) models suggest that opening the intellectual commons will spur development and promote a more equitable distribution of the world's resources. Developing countries, which lack strong domestic IPR-producing industries, often favor more open IPR systems that allow them to adopt, at minimal cost, technologies and IPR-rich products that are produced in the developed world. (pp. 101)

Sharing has become the primary principle of a new global political economy that promises to transform education and thereby also cultural and economic development. However, on the other side, sharing has become a killer application for the global economy in the face of decreased revenue streams. Goods that have been consumed in a noneconomic fashion, like cars via sharing agencies for students, are now monetized by companies like Uber with the bypassing of state regulations and taxes. It is a smart semantic move to call this the *Shareconomy*, thus capitalizing on a long tradition with roots going back to St. Martin's Day, that is, the Feast of St. Martin of Tours (316/317–397), that has been practiced throughout the centuries and within different societies without strict political rulings and economic incentives. Whereas the sharing of tools like drilling machines has been conducted in an informal way in closed communities, there are now global companies with platforms to exchange goods and services worldwide that portray a world where ownership is becoming less important. However, companies like Airbnb or Snapgoods are compromising the free market by subsidizing the supplier to compete with traditional providers, like taxi drivers in the case of Uber (Huet, 2014). The ultimate goal is to produce a market for every good possible and to push sharing into a strict economic logic, stripping down humanistic motives.

The general moral and philanthropic understanding of sharing has been utilized to advocate open educational resources (OER) that are based on other significant developments of openness in the digital era (open source, open access, open publishing). When the Massachusetts Institute of Technology (MIT) decided in 2002 to put most of its teaching and learning materials on the Internet with an open license, it was also the signal for a large movement that soon encompassed most parts of the world (OpenCourseWare Project, OCW) based on the idea of the Web as an open cultural space for unrestricted exchange of information so that "all can learn" (Bonk, 2009). In this regard, technology plays a crucial role, as it is portrayed as leverage to help equalize the distribution of high quality knowledge and educational opportunities for individuals. The goal of OER is thus to remove barriers in the free flow of information around the globe by utilizing a some-rights reserved model instead of the restricted all-rights reserved model. Individuals should not only have access to resources (retain) but also the ability to revise, reuse, remix and redistribute them. This is also reflected in the attempts of defining OER, for example, as

> teaching, learning and research materials in any medium, digital or otherwise, that reside in the public domain or have been released under an open license that permits no-cost access, use, adaptation and redistribution by others with no or limited restrictions. Open licensing is built within the existing framework of intellectual property rights as defined by relevant international conventions and respects the authorship of the work. (UNESCO, 2012)

In fact, the rather simple concept of OER—material that resides in the public domain or uses a free license—has contributed to its proliferation on platforms such as OCW because it is clearly distinctive against other free educational resources that do provide cost-free access but do not allow any alteration (e.g., on massive open online course [MOOC] platform Coursera). It also constitutes a major difference compared to previous forms of open education, such as open learning, open classroom or open curriculum, which were based on educational activism to the detriment of consistent and accountable standards regarding open practices. Yet without a clear definition, all of the promising attempts to change education failed, making way for a conservative backlash in the 1980s.

Over the last few years, there has been a considerable increase in funding for OER projects, most notably in the United States, which can partly be attributed to the enormous costs of textbooks. This has led to the open textbook movement, which aims at providing high-quality textbooks based on OER for students from lower income families. Research has also shown how beneficial low-budget textbooks and other open digital resources can be (Wiley, Hilton, Ellington, & Hall, 2012). Although providing affordable digital learning material is clearly a crucial step for a knowledge-based economy and society in general, there is also a need for more pedagogical and philosophical research to fully understand the potential of OER and open education (Deimann & Friesen, 2013).

One of the main advantages of OER is that these resources constitute a legal case for an open education ecology, which is based on a culture of sharing—which is opposed to the aforementioned Shareconomy. However, as important as it is to have unrestricted access to a broad variety of materials, this is not to be equated with the underlying process of education or Bildung, a form of self-realization and self-cultivation (Deimann & Sloep, 2013). The concept of MOOCs, which rose to prominence in 2012 when several high-profile universities opened their small-scaled classes to the general public over the Internet, served as a role model for open educational practices. With hundreds of thousands of learners enrolled in online courses, there has been tremendous media attention, causing headlines touting the coming revolution (Friedman, 2012) or the campus tsunami (Brooks, 2012). One of the core goals of open education seemed to be close to realization. Democratization of education and the claim of fairness of opportunities appeared to be achievable with the prospect of massive gains for the Global South and for the working poor in advanced countries. Yet, as more empirical evidence demonstrates, MOOCs and other forms of open online learning have affordances that severely interfere with their own claims; that is, the only learners who benefit from MOOCs are those who already have a college degree or those who are accustomed to learning in the open. Learners who lack prior knowledge and certain competences that are necessary to succeed are systematically left behind (Liyanagunawardena, Adams, & Williams, 2013).

These rather disappointing results have caused a debate of whether MOOCs really comprise such an adequate vision for the digital university and whether they provide adequate opportunities for establishing an open ecology of learning. In the time since, there has been a lot of experimentation around the initial MOOC categories to focus on specific pedagogic concepts, such as problem-based instruction. Other open courses reversed the first M and proclaimed a s(mall)MOOC. Nevertheless, MOOCs are still influential in the political realm and several reports build on the initial hype to argue for the transformation of higher education (European University Association, 2013). Openness is perceived as key leverage and is closely linked to economic growth by widening access to education. It seems also safe to assume that this recent trend of openness is much more sustainable than its ancestors from the 1960s and 1970s—there are now rather clear definitions of openness, for example in OER, which is beneficial for financial and political investments.

Although there have been distinctive variations of openness in education, the amount of self-reflection within education theory and philosophy is rather small. This may be attributable to the dynamic in which OER and MOOCs emerged, so it is too early for profound examination. Yet this pertains mostly to the technological infrastructure that enabled distribution of video and other multimedia content, whereas the very idea of openness is much older and has been dealt with in publications some decades ago (Barth, 1969). With the lack of interest in open education after the conservative backlash in the 1980s, there was a decline in theoretization, too.

Openness has emerged as a global logic based on free and open source software constituting a generalized response to knowledge capitalism and the attempt of the new mega-information utilities such as Google, Microsoft, and Amazon to control knowledge assets through the process of large-scale digitization of information that is often in the public domain, of the deployment of digital rights management regimes and of strong government lobbying to enforce intellectual property law in the international context. The Internet is a dynamic, open ecosystem that progressively changes its nature toward greater computing power, interactivity, inclusiveness, mobility, scale and peer governance. In this regard, and as the overall system develops, it begins to approximate the complexity of the architectures of natural ecosystems. The more it develops, one might be led to hypothesize, the greater the likelihood that it will not merely emulate Earth as a global ecosystem but will become an integrated organic whole. Open cultures become the necessary condition for the systems as a whole, for the design of open progressive technological improvements and their political, epistemic and ontological foundations.

Digitization transforms all aspects of cultural production and consumption, favoring the networked peer community over the individual author and blurring the distinction between writers, artists and their audiences. These new digital logics alter the traditional organization of knowledge, education and culture, spawning new technologies as a condition of the openness of the system. Now that the production of texts, sounds and images is open to new rounds of experimentation and development, a new grammar of digital culture is created. The processes of creativity are then transformed: They are no longer controlled by traditional knowledge institutions and organizations but are rather permitted by platforms and infrastructures that encourage large-scale participation and challenge old economic and political hierarchies. Every aspect of culture and economy is transformed through processes of digitization that create new systems of archives and representations and develop reproduction technologies that portend a Web 3.0 and Web 4.0, where all production—material and immaterial—will eventually be digitally designed and coordinated through distributed information systems and big data analytics.

With this book, we seek to revitalize previous attempts and to expand the field by focusing on the last decade and a half.

STRUCTURE OF THIS VOLUME

This edited volume consists of nine articles that have been submitted following personal invitations to experts in the field of open education. Each author has a specific research profile, and it was our goal to bring together those various standpoints. In keeping with the overall purpose of this book, the topics are grounded in philosophical and theoretical thinking, which sets them apart from the current emphasis on practical aspects (e.g., How to set up a technological infrastructure for OER in higher education). We very much hope that the exemplary collection will trigger a more substantial debate, as there are many more philosophically sound ways to engage with open education.

Robert Farrow opens the debate by asking the fundamentally obvious question: How can philosophy contribute to our understanding of openness? He goes on to argue that openness has been an issue in education for a long time (for an overview, see Peter & Deimann, 2013), but it would be "…mistaken to think that this represents a linear historical progression." Given the widespread usage of openness in education, which often—as in the case of MOOCs—lacks a common set of principles, Farrow proposes the concept of constellation, which is grounded in the work of Theodor Adorno. Constellations are understood as configurations of concepts, ideas, interpretations and historical patterns, and they offer a way to "…appreciate patterns of particularity as they emerge." Therefore, it is a helpful tool to embrace openness in a more nuanced way, which is beyond the current binary-coded discussions around the "battle for open" (Weller, 2014).

Michael Peters, in his chapter, "Openness and the Intellectual Commons," discusses the fundamental and ever-growing importance of openness for knowledge-based societies and especially for the realm of education. In his historical account, Peters argues that it was well before the Internet that openness was used in technologically sophisticated ways to ensure that the delivery of education is not restricted in terms of location or study time. Yet when the Internet emerged as a global cultural phenomenon, the concept of intellectual commons also was raised as a viable alternative to the dominant knowledge capitalism. Liberally licensed materials (OER) and multiple ways to distribute this content and connect people worldwide gave cause for a new open education movement.

Petra Missomelius and Theo Hug focus on the fundamental educational question: "How is 'education' understood in the OER movement and what effects concerning education in media cultures are to be expected from the newest trends?" They do so by taking a position that builds on media theory, educational philosophy and metatheoretical considerations. This helps to build a broader framework of media ecologies to critically discuss recent developments in open education. One aspect pertains to the predominant focus of providing free and open access to educational materials, which is to the detriment of the process of supporting learners.

David Small discusses the role of the university in terms of MOOCs and neoliberalism as two major ways of change emerging during the last decades. MOOCs, which are often portrayed as a game changer for more affordable education, are understood as a symbolic development that challenge the way universities work. It is argued that the ongoing restructuring of universities as players in the educational marketplace provides fertile ground for MOOCs following a rather conservative epistemology. Therefore, deeper philosophical and political questions that arise during the implementation of MOOCs are neglected, which influences the future of the university.

Jeremy Knox attempts to look beyond technology instrumentalism, which he terms *posthuman openings*. His main argument is a criticism of the predominant narrative of education that sees the humanist subject as an independent agent based on essentialism, universalism and autonomy. It is this form of subject in which MOOCs, both in the reductionist (xMOOC) as well as in the connectivistic version, are targeted. Yet it does only account for one side and neglects the material component of studying online. A posthuman position is therefore suggested to deconstruct the humanistic framework and to account for the agency of the material. Using a case study of two MOOCs, Knox outlines the implications of an expanded perspective of sociomaterial spaces.

Peter Sloep and Robert Schuwer tackle an important issue that has become apparent in recent approaches of open education. The offering of open access to high-quality content may be motivated by two contrasting philosophies. The first is related to the old tradition of humanistic education (Bildung), which has been manifested, for instance, in the foundation of open universities. The other is inspired by the disruption narrative that has emerged within Silicon Valley, where a strong techno-determinism made numerous start-ups to provide "solutions" for some of the most urgent problems in our society, among them education. These enterprises are specialized in the distribution of content on a global scale (MOOCs) and do not care about the support of learners. They justify their organization as a step toward democratization of education, but this could also be understood as a form of liberal capitalist utilitarianism. Sloep and Schuwer argue that we are at the crossroads regarding the kind of openness we want in education, and they lay out a set of reasons why we should strive for a humanitarian approach.

In the chapter titled "Another World Is Possible: The Relationship Between Open Higher Education and Mass Intellectuality," Richard Hall takes on the increasing exploitation of open education (most notably MOOCs) by economically driven organizations, which is enframed in a global transformation of higher education toward marketization and financialization. He then introduces the concept of mass intellectuality as a countermeasure to revitalize noneconomic traditions of open education, such as cooperative organizing principles (e.g., sharing).

Martin Oliver provides an account on open access, freedom and exclusion. He starts with the observation that the increasing access to (educational) materials on the Internet alters the perception of education toward a matter of information flow and thus pushes teaching to the background. He argues that an effect of the neoliberal transformation of the educational system is that the freedom not to access resources slips away. On the other hand, open educational practices constitute a new form of tether: Whereas in the traditional form, the student had to go to the campus to receive education via lectures or by visiting the library, it is now possible to access digital content via mobile phones.

Michael Peters, Richard Heraud and Andrew Gibbons provide a broad account of openness that is based on several transformations in different realms of society (open government, open data, open science) and argue that this has ushered in new ways of thinking about education. Yet there is also a much older understanding of openness that can be traced back to the Enlightenment, which inspired experimentations of alternative architecture in schools. With the rise of modern information and communications technology (ICT), open education has been on the forefront of implementing these tools and software, as they quickly realized their potential to bring learning content or learning management systems to the masses. The authors then switch to the topic of social production and social innovation as a new playground for the culture of openness.

REFERENCES

Barth, R. S. (1969). Open education—Assumptions about learning. *Educational Philosophy and Theory, 1*(2), 29–39.

Bonk, C. (2009). *The world is open: How web technology is revolutionizing education.* San Francisco, CA: Jossey-Bass.

Brooks, D. (2012, May 3). The campus tsunami. *New York Times.* New York. Retrieved from http://www.nytimes.com/2012/05/04/opinion/brooks-the-campus-tsunami.html?_r=0

Deimann, M., & Friesen, N. (2013). Introduction. Exploring the educational potential of open educational resources. *E-Learning and Digital Media, 10*(2), 112–115.

Deimann, M., & Sloep, P. (2013). How does open education work? In A. Meiszner & L. Squires (Eds.), *Openness and education: Advances in digital education and lifelong learning* (Vol. 1, pp. 1–23). Bingley, UK: Emerald.

European University Association. (2013, October 18). *Making sense of the MOOCs.* Report from ACA-EUA Seminar in Brussels. Retrieved from http://www.eua.be/News/13-10-18/Making_sense_of_the_MOOCs_-_report_from_ACA-EUA_Seminar_in_Brussels_10_October.aspx

Friedman, T. (2012, May 15). Come the revolution. *New York Times.* New York. Retrieved from http://www.nytimes.com/2012/05/16/opinion/friedman-come-the-revolution.html

Huet, E. (2014, July 2). Uber's newest tactic: Pay drivers more than they earn. *Forbes.* Retrieved from http://www.forbes.com/sites/ellenhuet/2014/07/02/ubers-newest-tactic-pay-drivers-more-than-they-earn/

Liyanagunawardena, T. R., Adams, A. A., & Williams, S. A. (2013). MOOCs: A systematic study of the published literature 2008–2012. *International Review of Research in Open and Distance Learning, 14*(3), 202–227.

Mill, J. S. (2002, November 29). Freedom of speech. *Stanford Encyclopedia of Philosophy.* Retrieved from http://plato.stanford.edu/entries/freedom-speech/

Moldoveanu, M. C. (2000). Foundations of the open society: Discourse ethics and the logic of inquiry. *Journal of Socio-Economics, 29,* 403–442. Retrieved from https://www.researchgate.net/profile/

Mihnea_Moldoveanu/publication/223532875_Foundations_of_the_open_society_discourse_ethics_and_the_logic_of_inquiry/links/02bfe51238d3d5e5d4000000.pdf

Momigliano, A. (2003). Freedom of speech in antiquity. In P. P. Wiener (Ed.), *Dictionary of the history of ideas* (pp. 252–263). Charlottesville: University of Virginia. (Original work published 1973)

Opderbeck, D. W. (2007). The penguin's paradox: The political economy of international intellectual property and the paradox of open intellectual property models. *Stanford Law and Policy Review, 18*, 101–160.

Peter, S., & Deimann, M. (2013). On the role of openness in education: A historical reconstruction. *Open Praxis, 5*(1), 1–8.

Peters, M., & Bulut, E. (Hrsg.). (2011). *Cognitive capitalism, education, and digital labor.* New York: Peter Lang.

Popper, K. R. (1945). *The open society and its enemies.* London, UK: Routledge.

Thake, W. (2004). Editing and the crisis of open source. *M/C: A Journal of Media and Culture, 7*(3), b1–b2. Retrieved from http://journal.media-culture.org.au/0406/04_Thake.php

UNESCO. (2012, June 22). *The Paris Declaration.* Retrieved from http://www.unesco.org/new/filead min/MULTIMEDIA/HQ/CI/CI/pdf/Events/Paris%20OER%20Declaration_01.pdf

Weller, M. (2014). *The battle for open: How openness won and why it doesn't feel like victory.* London, UK: Ubiquity Press.

Wiley, D., Hilton III, J. L., Ellington, S., & Hall, T. (2012). A preliminary examination of the cost savings and learning impacts of using open textbooks in middle and high school science classes. *International Review of Research in Open and Distance Learning, 13*(3), 262–276.

CHAPTER ONE

Constellations OF Openness

ROBERT FARROW

THE AMBIGUITY OF PROGRESS

There have always been tensions and philosophical questions provoked by the idea of open education. Peter and Deimann (2013) have demonstrated that the history of openness can be understood to stretch back before the institutionalization of education, even if the language of open was not always used. In their reconstruction of the process of widening access to education they trace the gradual expansion of educational opportunity through the cathedral schools of the Middle Ages and Gutenberg's invention of the printing press. With industrialization came the rise of popular literacy and the establishment of public libraries and opportunities for distance education. The 20th century has continued to see an extension of the belief that education was a right that could be extended to all. Yet it is mistaken to think that this represents a linear historical progression. Instead we discern complex patterns of economic and social change in a dialectical relationship with an evolving understanding of openness. The authors make the observation that "historical forms of openness caution us against assuming that particular configurations will prevail, or that social aspects should be assumed as desired by default" (Peter & Deimann, 2013, p. 12).

Increasingly, it is the social and cultural implications of openness that draw the attention of scholars. The American philosopher of education John Dewey was among the first of the moderns to advocate a holistic view of education which emphasized learning beyond the classroom and established curriculum. Henderson (1957) argued the following:

> It is doubtful whether many teachers really understood the…philosophical foundations. Certainly, few had studied Dewey's philosophy against any background of other philosophies…. To some extent the movement was popular because it constituted a revolt against the boring formalism of the traditional school. (p. 250)

By the 1960s the open education movement had begun to coalesce around the idea of disestablishing cultural, economic and institutional barriers to formal education. The Open University in the United Kingdom was founded in 1969 to widen access to higher education by disregarding the need for prior academic qualification and using the communication technologies of the time to 'open up' campus education though a "teaching system to suit an individual working in a lighthouse off the coast of Scotland" (Daniel, Kanwar, & West, 2008).

Open universities, now commonly found all around the world, have massively expanded access to education. Over the last decade—primarily in the form of massive open online courses (MOOCs) and open educational resources (OER)—the open education movement has further expanded opportunities for education worldwide. Yet as opportunities for accessing educational materials increases, so higher education (in the West, at least) has increasingly seemed to be in a crisis of funding shortfalls, massive student debt and a lack of graduate employment. This has led some to ask whether open education is the saviour of traditional education or the herald of its demise.

> One question asked of the free approach is whether or not it can be sustained without obvious business models that match income to resources. Rather the question that should be first considered is whether the existing models can be sustained in the face of the global demand, limited resources and the alternatives that are available? In those terms the free and open case may be the only answer that is genuinely sustainable through its ability to incorporate distribution and diversity. (McAndrew, 2010)

FORMS OF OPENNESS

Arriving at correct definitions of words and ideas has been a key challenge for philosophy since the Ancients. Indeed, the Socratic method described by Plato can be understood to begin from the interrogation of a key concept such as justice (as in Book 1 of *Republic;* Plato, 2008b) or beauty (*Phaedo* 100b–102d; Plato, 2008a), with the eventual aim of uncovering the essence of that concept through dialogue. So influential has this approach become that it has characterised all philosophy that followed. In Whitehead's (1929) famous remark, "the safest general characterization of the European philosophical tradition is that it consists of a series of footnotes to Plato" (p. 39). Definitions continue to be important for approaching philosophical questions and for establishing the truth of propositions. Definitions can also be integral to ideological positions and thus inform the activities of communities of practice (Lave & Wenger, 1991; Veenswijk & Chisalita, 2007).

How then can philosophy contribute to our understanding of openness? As it once more moves to the foreground of debates about the future of education, there remain tensions in our collective understanding of what openness in education might mean. As Weller (2014) described it, the 'battle for open' is won and yet the present situation does not feel like victory.

> Open approaches are featured in the mainstream media. Millions of people are enhancing their learning through open resources and open courses. Put bluntly, it looks as though openness has won. And yet you would be hard pressed to find any signs of celebration amongst those original advocates. They are despondent about the reinterpretation of openness to mean 'free' or 'online' without some of the reuse liberties they had envisaged. Concerns are expressed about the commercial interests that are now using openness as a marketing tool. Doubts are raised regarding the benefits of some open models for developing nations or learners who require support. At this very moment of victory it seems that the narrative around openness is being usurped by others, and the consequences of this may not be very open at all. (Weller, 2014, p. 14)

Many different interpretations of openness have been advanced, often favouring one or more elements at the expense of others. As the Internet has made possible the widespread sharing of educational materials at marginal cost, so openness has become a greater focus of attention in education. The archetypal contemporary realisations of the idea of openness in education are perhaps the forms of OER and MOOC, though there are other noteworthy examples. Perhaps the most widespread understanding of openness is *open access* publication: making peer reviewed research available free of charge and with minimal copyright and other licensing restrictions (Suber, 2012). Open access comes in two variants: *gratis* (free online access) and *libre* (as *gratis* but with additional free online access plus some usage rights around reproducing scholarly work).

Much attention has been devoted to defining OER, with different underlying understandings of 'open.' For many, the issue is the licence applied to a resource. The UNESCO (2002) forum on the impact of open courseware for higher education in developing countries offered one of the first attempts to define OER: "teaching, learning and research materials in any medium, digital or otherwise, that reside in the public domain or have been released under an open license that permits no-cost access, use, adaptation and redistribution by others with no or limited restrictions."

At their most general, "open educational resources are materials used to support education that may be freely accessed, reused, modified and shared by anyone" (Downes, 2011), or they are "teaching, learning, and research resources that reside in the public domain or have been released under an intellectual property license that permits their free use and re-purposing by others" (Hewlett Foundation, n.d.). Yet not all open licences support all of these possibilities: They may, for instance, prohibit commercial use of a resource. As Wiley (2014) noted, any restrictions on use increase the 'friction' involved in working with open content. It is also possible to place an unrestrictive licence on a resource and then fail to effectively share it. Does such a resource deserve to be described as open? If not, then the openness of a resource describes a context of use and cannot be reduced to a matter of licensing.

With MOOCs and their various derivatives, 'open' tends to denote courses which can be joined by anyone who has the appropriate technology to access content delivered online—there are no requirements for prior qualification. This has led to some courses having hundreds of thousands of registered learners, with an average enrollment of around 40,000 students (Jordan, 2014). MOOCs have often been described as either cMOOCs or xMOOCs. cMOOCs originally ran to test connectivist theories about networked learning through processes of accumulation, collective content creation and sharing (Siemens, 2005). Most large course numbers—sometimes with hundreds of thousands of learners—are found in xMOOCs, which typically make institutional course content available to large numbers of learners, but they have been accused of being pedagogically backward (Stacey, 2014). As Bayne and Ross (2014, pp. 21–22) noted, we are starting to see a move away from the cMOOC/xMOOC binary and greater recognition of more diverse forms of open online courses, including DOCC (distributed open collaborative course), POOC (participatory open online course), BOOC (big/boutique/badged open online course) and even a non-open variant—SPOC (small private online course).

MOOCs generate large amounts of data on their students, and these data have become a focus of interest, with some suggesting that they should be shared under an open licence to improve learning analytics. Other forms of *open data* in education include research and government data that are shared for use in teaching and learning. *Open pedagogy* was defined by Wiley (2013) as "that set of teaching and learning practices only possible in the context of the free access and [the] permissions characteristic of open educational resources." Implicit here is the idea that openness should make some difference to the way people teach and learn—OER should function as "radical objects" (McAndrew & Farrow, 2013, p. 74). DS106, which began at the University of Mary Washington and now continues as an online community, is often held up as an example of a radically open pedagogy (Levine, 2013). Other forms of *open educational practices* include a whole life cycle of OER production and use, institutional strategies, the empowerment of informal learners, the creation of environments that support learning and the empowerment of individuals (Ehlers, 2013, pp. 89–97). In addition, *open policy*—the view that all publicly funded resources should be openly licensed—has been proposed as a way of increasing the supply of open content (Wiley & Green, 2012).

We might also note that the rhetoric of openness also extends beyond education. Examples here include open government (more transparent, inclusive processes of policy making), open source software, open hardware and open design. It is beyond the scope of this chapter to explore all of these different elements, but we can at least note that they are highly diverse and reflect many different interests and elements of society. Openness can be seen as a matter of access, of licence, of publicity, of pedagogical practice or of policy, and yet it is not reducible to any one of these. Sometimes it seems to refer to processes and sometimes to the outcomes of those processes. Nonetheless, it remains hard to give up on the possibility that something unites all of these aspects of openness. Atenas and Havemann (2014) commented: "Notwithstanding the problematic nature of the term 'open' when used in wider contexts, there does seem to be a shared understanding of an underlying ethos of openness…."

At the same time, the possibility of a final definition of openness remains elusive, sublime and perhaps forever out of reach. Why should this be? A likely clue is in the word 'open' and its versatility as a concept.

> An excellent candidate for sloganizing is the word 'open.' Immediately one uses it, the options polarize. To be open (depending on context) is to be not closed, restricted, prejudiced or clogged; but free, candid, generous, above board, mentally flexible, future oriented. (Hill, 1975/2010, p. 2)

In one sense this quote illustrates the particularities of the concept of openness. Complete openness is also complete emptiness: It has no real essence of its own but is characterised instead by its potentiality. In educational practice, of course, we tend to use 'open' to refer to something that defines itself against a status quo, which places some restriction on activity—such as who gets to learn, and how, and who decides what curriculum will be followed and which resources will be used. Definitions of openness are typically concerned with the removal of restrictions to activities like sharing resources and data in particular ways rather than the establishment of what Isaiah Berlin (1969/2002) termed 'positive freedom'—the autonomy judgement required to meaningfully direct one's agency. 'Open access' simply refers to publications that can be accessed freely. 'Open educational resources' are resources that can be treated in any way one desires: copied, adapted and otherwise manipulated. 'Open data' can be downloaded and analysed by anyone. 'Open courses' can be joined by anyone with access to the requisite technology. 'Open source' software development provides universal access to source code which can be adapted, improved and further shared without violating copyright. In each of these cases, openness really refers to the removal of a barrier that previously impeded some groups from participation.

With this is mind we must ask the following: Can there really be an essence of openness? If, as I have suggested, open merely amounts to a kind of negative liberty, is that similar to an abscence of externally imposed restraint? Can we describe openness (as absence of restriction) in ways which are amenable to practical application and can inform pedagogical strategies and policy making? And what is at stake in the debate around 'genuine' and 'nongenuine' forms of openness? For if we deny that there is a common essence of openness, then it surely becomes much more difficult to distinguish authentic and inauthentic forms.

AUTHENTICITY AND OPENNESS

As far back as the 1970s, the argument was being made that 'open education' was a somewhat nebulous phrase (Denton, 1975; Hyland, 1979). More recently, Weller (2014, p. 31) has argued that the multiplicity of possible interpretations of open are attractive because they allow for widespread adoption, but this flexibility is also capable of being claimed by those whose motives are, for instance, commercial.

> Not only are there different aspects of openness, but it may be that some are mutually exclusive with others, or at least that prioritising some means less emphasis on others. One way to consider openness is to consider the motivations people have for adopting an open approach. (Weller, 2014, p. 32)

Motives for embracing the epithet 'open' vary widely. Though profit motive and the desire to educate can coexist, the encroachment of commercial organizations into the landscape of openness has been considered quite provocative by core members of the open education movement. Part of the difficulty here is that what makes an educational resource 'open' remains vague and thus open to abuse or misrepresentation. Such misuse is typically associated with commercial publishers and e-learning providers who use this language to describe a product that is essentially proprietary and intended primarily to make a profit by using 'open' to increase the appeal of a brand. 'Open' here functions as little more than public relations or a marketing tool—what has been termed 'openwashing' after the 'greenwashing' phenomenon associated with the attempt by corporations to brand themselves as environmentally friendly as the green movement began to gain popularity (Weller, 2014; Wiley, 2011). Commercial organisations now commonly describe their virtual learning environments, textbooks, supplementary materials, and so on, as 'open.' Audrey Watters (2014) made the following remark at OpenCon2014:

> I can list for you any number of examples of companies and organizations that have attached that word "open" to their products and services: OpenClass, an [sic] learning management system built by Pearson…. The Open Education Alliance—an industry group founded by the online education startup Udacity…. The startup Open English, an online English-language learning site and one of the most highly funded startups in the last few years. I don't know what "open" refers to there in Open English. All these append "open" to a name without really even trying to append "openness," let alone embrace "openness," to their practices or mission. Whatever "openness" means. (para. 7)

Commercial appropriation of the idea of openness is the clearest example of where the authenticity of the movement is called into question. But there are a range of other examples. These include issues around the following:

- *Pedagogy:* lack of clarity around what constitutes an open approach and competing ideas about how to achieve this.
- *Technology:* around licensing; technologies for content storage and delivery; accessibility and usability.
- *Ethics:* concerned with publicity, open release of data; open access publication; access to education.
- *Politics:* concerning the establishment of a consensus around definitions and use cases; advocacy; disruption of established business models.

These challenges can be characterized as questions of epistemological and linguistic authority, reducible to reflection on who decides the meaning of 'open' and whether there is a possibility of reliably distinguishing authentic or 'pure' forms of openness from their inauthentic or false equivalents.

PRACTICAL APPROACHES TO THE PROBLEM OF DEFINITION

One way to approach the complexities of defining openness is to adopt a purely practical stance. For instance, we might adapt Ludwig Wittgenstein's later arguments about the pragmatic and contextual essence of meaningful language. He argued that concepts can be meaningful without being clearly defined. Vagueness is part of natural language, and the rules for the use of a word are largely determined by the way it is used. So we should focus on the way language is used practically if we want to understand it (Wittgenstein, 1953, sec. 43), which Wittgenstein showed through the idea of a "family resemblance" [*Familienähnlichkeit*] between different practical uses and associations of the word (Wittgenstein, 1953, sec. 2, pp. 65–67). The meaning of language is fundamentally rooted in practice, or "forms of life" [*Lebensform*].

In essence, this pragmatic stance is taken up by the majority of those working in open education, keen to make progress instead of endlessly philosophising about definitions. There is a practical virtue to this approach, since 'open' is used in so many different ways. But Wittgenstein is also clear that we should not give up on the idea of tight or final definitions. Rather, we need to be aware of the fact that 'defining' is also a language game [*Sprachspiel*] with its own pragmatic rules and logic. We nonetheless need ways to differentiate and better understand different patterns of openness as a method for improving our understanding of the ethos of openness.

A purely pragmatic approach based in contextual activity is perfectly justifiable but risks unreflective disengagement from important theoretical considerations, or mistaking the part for the whole. Such a strategy may also overlook dialectical aspects of the relationship between theory and practice in favour of achieving predetermined goals. Some may also mistake such an approach for relativism: Why should your idea of open match mine when our practices are not the same? In addition, without a clear sense of what is meant by openness, it becomes harder to effectively understand the impact of educational interventions that call themselves 'open.' What is needed, then, is a way of unpacking the idea of openness which is grounded in practice, nonreductive, and provides enough of a framework to make wider insights possible.

OPENNESS AS *CONSTELLATION*

To provide such a framework, I propose to appropriate from Frankfurt School critical theorists (particularly Theodor Adorno) the methodological perspective of 'constellation.' Critical theories of society attempt to give an account of what is wrong (or bad) about (or in) the social world by considering the whole in its historical specificity. The Frankfurt School grew into being during the rise of National Socialism in Germany and attempted to explain the contemporary forms of social domination: state capitalism, propaganda, centralization of power, totalitarianism and fascism. The development of the distinctive approach can be traced back to the perception that the historical predictions of classical Marxism were not being realised. The distinctive focus of the Frankfurt School was on the role of false consciousness and "ideology in the strict sense" in the perpetuation of capitalism (Horkheimer, 1936/1973, p. 211).

Because ideology affects the categories within which we think—essentially, ideology determines limits to thought—we cannot access nonideological thought directly. Adorno borrowed from the cultural critic Walter Benjamin the idea that inaccessible truths become comprehensible through the 'constellation' [*Konstellation*]: the configuration of concepts, ideas, interpretations and historical patterns which provides insights into the uniqueness of the object of thought (in this case, openness) without necessitating the claim to have complete knowledge or understanding of it. The object of thought becomes better understood in its particularity: "Ideas are to objects as constellations are to stars" (Benjamin, 1985b, p. 34). Through critical reflection it is 'unlocked' from its context: "As a constellation, theoretical thought circles around the concept it would like to unseal, hoping that it may fly open like the lock of a well-guarded safe" (Adorno, 1962/1973, p. 163).

Adorno's thought is notoriously complex, and to elucidate further aspects of his approach would take us far from the matter under discussion. What does the idea of 'constellation' mean for understanding forms of openness? Instead of thinking of openness as a binary or totalizing category, we should appreciate patterns of particularity as they emerge: what Jay (1984, p. 15) referred to as "a juxtaposed rather than integrated cluster of changing elements that resist reduction to a common denominator, essential core, or generative first principle." It is this juxtaposition of fragments which exposes tensions in diverse phenomena by bringing them 'together.' Thus the very act of "setting [concepts] in constellation…illuminates what is specific to the thing, to which the classificatory system is indifferent" (Adorno, 1962/1973, p. 162).

It is through historical processes that (often fleeting) constellations come into being. As I argued earlier, different elements of openness are revealed by different practices and discourses. Seeing them 'in constellation' provides a critical framework which recognizes and values the ongoing need for clearer and more insightful definitions relating to practice. By emphasising the networked and relational nature of openness in action, an ongoing and iterative attempt to rethink the teleological assumptions implied by different uses of the term 'open' is enhanced. Adorno also counsels us to move beyond the polarizing, binary judgements (open or not) implied by essentialism: "The constellation of moments," he wrote, "is not to be reduced to a singular essence; what is inherent in that constellation is not an essence" (Adorno, 1962/1973, p. 104). In this way we focus on historical contingency so that fragments of evidence "'gather around' the unique history of the object where this history makes the object the unique thing that it is" (Stone, 2008, p. 59). This allows us to recognise historical contingency without recourse to oversimplification or relativism, being guided by real and existing practice. Crucially, the constellation methodology begins from specific, actually existing instances of openness. The existence of one constellation does not prohibit the possibility of other interpretations, other constellations which are disclosed through both continuity and discontinuity with previous forms. This distinguishes the approach from a relativism that treats all interpretations of openness as of equal epistemic worth.

In practical terms, what does this amount to? The method of constellation is intimately related to how we use language and how language influences thought (Adorno, 1974, p. 162). We need to move on from thinking of openness as a binary value and appreciate that *openness is always contextual*. We need to interrogate the ways we use language to organize education and the kinds of assumptions we make about what is valid. We should always be trying to make our language as precise as possible and be wary of differentiating authentic and nonauthentic forms of openness on the basis of any one axiom like licensing, or patterns of access.

CONCLUSION

This chapter has attempted to provide a more philosophically nuanced account of the relation among different examples of openness in education through a framework adapted from Adorno's notion of 'constellation.' The 'ecosystem' metaphor has often been applied to the emergent world of open education, and the Adornian concept of constellation provides a rigorous theoretical basis for unpacking this concept and the critical tools for assessing and critiquing educational interventions.

Openness should not be viewed as a binary quality, as a panacea, or as a 'magic' category that can be used to evaluate all aspects of educational systems. Openness may not even be the most important element of any education system, but the outward-facing and reflexive aspects of genuine openness can act as a normative keystone in our attempts to better understand the pedagogical systems of the future.

I have argued that openness has no essence because it is fundamentally the removal of some barrier to activity (and hence, always 'negative' in Berlin's sense). One implication of this is that openness should be understood as orientated toward a state of pure freedom where all imposed barriers to activity are overcome. That said, the open education movement needs to articulate a stronger sense of the positive freedoms of openness. This could involve making stronger ideological claims about the ethical basis of open education or explicitly endorsing a vision of social justice while arguing that this is part of what it means to be open. Through a transition like this, we may even eventually stop using the word 'open' altogether. Eventually the rhetoric of openness may give way to a new and more substantive rubric of educational freedoms, but in lieu of this, by its very indeterminate nature, openness inevitably retains the possibility that it will become "a theatre of new, unforeseen constellations" (Benjamin, 1985a, p. 169) in education.

REFERENCES

Adorno, T. W. (1973). *Negative dialectics*. New York, NY: Routledge. (Original work published 1962).
Atenas, J., & Havemann, L. (2014). Questions of quality in repositories of open educational resources: A literature review [Special issue]. *Research in Learning Technology, 22*. Retrieved from http://www.researchinlearningtechnology.net/index.php/rlt/article/view/20889

Bayne, S., & Ross, J. (2014). The pedagogy of the massive open online course (MOOC): The UK view. *Higher Education Academy*. Retrieved from https://www.heacademy.ac.uk/resources/detail/elt/the_pedagogy_of_the_MOOC_UK_view

Benjamin, W. (1985a). *One-way street and other writings* (E. Jephcott & K. Shorter, Trans.). London, UK: Verso.

Benjamin, W. (1985b). *The origin of German tragic drama* (J. Osbourne, Trans.). London, UK: Verso.

Berlin, I. (2002). Two concepts of liberty. In I. Berlin (Ed.), *Four essays on liberty*. London, UK: Oxford University Press. (Original work published 1969)

Creative Commons. (2013). *What is OER?* Retrieved from http://wiki.creativecommons.org/What_is_OER%3F

Daniel, J., Kanwar, S., & West, P. (2008). Distance education across borders. *Asian Association of Open Universities*. Retrieved from http://oasis.col.org/bitstream/handle/11599/1234/2008_Daniel_Distance_Borders_Transcript.pdf?sequence=1&isAllowed=y

Denton, D. E. (1975). Open education: Search for a new myth. *Educational Theory, 25*, 397–406. doi:10.1111/j.1741-5446.1975.tb00703.x.

Downes, S. (2011). Open educational resources: A definition. *Half an Hour*. Retrieved from http://halfanhour.blogspot.co.uk/2011/07/open-educational-resources-definition.html

Ehlers, U-D. (2013). *Open learning cultures: A guide to quality, evaluation, and assessment for future learning*. Heidelberg, Germany: Springer Science & Business Media.

Henderson, S. v. P. (1957). *Introduction to the philosophy of education*. Chicago, IL: The University of Chicago Press.

Hewlett Foundation. (n.d.). Open educational resources. Retrieved from http://www.hewlett.org/programs/education/open-educational-resources

Hill, B. V. (2010). What's open about open education? In D. A. Nyberg (Ed.), *The philosophy of open education*. New York, NY: Routledge. (Original work published 1975)

Horkheimer, M. (1973). Traditional and critical theory. In M. J. O'Connell (Ed.), *Critical theory* (pp. 188–214). New York, NY: Herder & Herder. (Original work published 1936)

Hyland, J. T. (1979). Open education: A slogan examined. *Educational Studies, 5*(1), 35–41.

Jay, M. (1984). *Adorno*. Cambridge, MA: Harvard University Press.

Jordan, K. (2014). Initial trends in enrolment and completion of massive open online courses. *The International Review of Research in Open and Distributed Learning, 15*(1), 133–160. Retrieved from http://www.irrodl.org/index.php/irrodl/article/view/1651

Lave, J., & Wenger, E. (1991). *Situated learning: Legitimate peripheral participation*. Cambridge, UK: Cambridge University Press.

Levine, A. (2013). ds106: Not a course, not like any MOOC. *Educause Review, 48*(1), 54–55.

McAndrew, P. (2010). Defining openness: Updating the concept of "open" for a connected world. *Journal of Interactive Media in Education, 2010*(2), 10. Retrieved from http://dx.doi.org/10.5334/2010-10

McAndrew, P., & Farrow, R. (2013). Open education research: From the practical to the theoretical. In R. McGreal, W. Kinuthia, & S. Marshall (Eds.), *Open educational resources: Innovation, research and practice* (pp. 65–78). Vancouver, Canada: Commonwealth of Learning and Athabasca University.

Peter, S., & Deimann, M. (2013). On the role of openness in education: A historical reconstruction. *Open Praxis, 5*(1), 7–14. doi:10.5944/openpraxis.5.1.23

Plato. (2008a). *Phaedo* (B. Jowett, Trans.). Retrieved from http://www.gutenberg.org/files/1658/1658-h/1658-h.htm

Plato. (2008b). *Republic* (B. Jowett, Trans.). Retrieved from http://www.gutenberg.org/files/1497/1497-h/1497-h.htm

Siemens, G. (2005). Connectivism: A learning theory for the digital age. *International Journal of Instructional Technology and Distance Learning, 2*(1), 3–10.

Stacey, P. (2014). Pedagogy of MOOCs. *The International Journal for Innovation and Quality in Learning, 2*(3), 111–115.

Stone, A. (2008). Adorno and logic. In D. Cook (Ed.), *Theodor Adorno: Key concepts* (pp. 47–62). Stocksfield, UK: Acumen.

Suber, P. (2012). *Open access.* Cambridge, MA: The MIT Press.

UNESCO. (2002, July). *Forum on the impact of open courseware for higher education in developing countries: Final report.* Retrieved from http://unesdoc.unesco.org/images/0012/001285/128515e.pdf

Veenswijk, M., & Chisalita, C. M. (2007). The importance of power and ideology in communities of practice: The case of a de-marginalized user interface design team in a failing multi-national design company. *Information Technology & People, 20*(1), 32–52.

Watters, A. (2014, November 15). *From "open" to justice: OpenCon 2014.* Retrieved from http://hackeducation.com/2014/11/16/from-open-to-justice/

Weller, M. (2014). *Battle for open: How openness won and why it doesn't feel like victory.* London, UK: Ubiquity Press. Retrieved from http://dx.doi.org/10.5334/bam

Whitehead, A. N. (1929). *Process and reality.* New York, NY: Simon & Schuster.

Wiley, D. (2011, July 27). Openwashing—The new greenwashing. *iterating toward openness.* Retrieved from http://opencontent.org/blog/archives/1934

Wiley, D. (2013, October 21). What is open pedagogy? *iterating toward openness.* Retrieved from http://opencontent.org/blog/archives/2975

Wiley, D. (2014, August 1). Refining the definition of "open" in open content. *iterating toward openness.* Retrieved from http://opencontent.org/blog/archives/3442

Wiley, D., & Green, C. (2012). Why openness in education? In D. G. Oblinger (Ed.), *Game changers: Education and information technologies* (pp. 81–90). Washington, DC: Educause. Retrieved from http://net.educause.edu/ir/library/pdf/pub7203.pdf

Wittgenstein, L. (1953). *Philosophical investigations* (G. E. M. Anscombe & R. Rhees, Eds.; G. E. M. Anscombe, Trans.). Oxford, UK: Blackwell.

CHAPTER TWO

Openness AND THE Intellectual Commons

MICHAEL A. PETERS

'Openness' is one of the central contested values of modern liberal society and falls under different political descriptions. In this chapter I employ 'openness' to signal and introduce a new spatialization, interconnectivity, mobility, personalization and globalization of learning and education.

The dimensions of openness and 'open education' (Peters & Britez, 2008) found a beginning in education with the concept of The Open University as it developed in the United Kingdom (UK) during the 1960s. The concept of openness considered in the light of the new 'technologies of openness' of Web 2.0 promises to promote interactivity and encourage participation and collaboration and help to establish new forms of the intellectual commons now increasingly based on models of open source, open access, open archives and open education. Where the former is based on the logic of centralized industrial mass media characterized by a broadcast one-to-many mode, the latter is based upon a radically decentralized, 'many-to-many' mode of interactivity. To exemplify the progress and possibilities of this second possibility we might examine Massachusetts Institute of Technology's (MIT's) OpenCourseWare and Harvard's open access initiative to publicly post its faculty's papers online. The real and immediate possibilities of a form of openness that combines the benefits of these first two forms provides a means to investigate the political economy of openness as it reconfigures higher education in the knowledge economy of the 21st century.

The underlying argument of this editorial focuses upon the ways in which new forms of technological-enabled openness, especially emergent social media that utilizes social networking, blogs, wikis and user-created content and media, provide new models of openness for a conception of the intellectual commons based on peer production, which is a radically decentralized, genuinely interactive and collaborative form of knowledge sharing that can usefully serve as the basis of 'knowledge cultures' (Peters & Besley, 2006; Peters & Roberts, 2011). The first concept of openness was based on social democratic principles that emphasized inclusiveness and equality of opportunity. The mechanism of this notion of openness followed that of industrial broadcast mass media, which was designed to reach a large audience on a one-to-many logic. The second form of openness is based on what might be called principles of liberal political economy, particularly intellectual property and freedom of information. This second iteration of openness employs new peer-to-peer architectures and technologies that are part of the ideology of Web 2.0 and given expression in ways that emphasize the ethic of participation ('participatory media'), collaboration and file-sharing characterizing the rise of social media.

This new form of openness provides the basis for a new social media model of the university that embraces the social democratic articles of the original Open University and provides the means to recover and enhance the historical mission of the university in the 21st century (Peters, 2006). It also provides mechanisms for jettisoning the dominant neoliberal managerialist ideology and returning to a fully socialized view of knowledge and knowledge sharing that has its roots in Enlightenment thinking about science and its new practices in commons-based peer production. At the same time, however, I recognize that any re-theorization of the university must move beyond the limitations of even this form that—despite its logic of openness—often coheres around exclusive institutions such as MIT and Harvard and is correspondingly reliant on factors of exclusivity, including intellectual property and the privileging of 'expertise.' Consequently, the development of openness as it relates to the university must move from the social democratic model of the first concept, and the liberal political economy model of the second, to a new version of openness based on the 'intellectual commons.' Only through such a development might this new institutional possibility achieve its potential as a locus of true social and intellectual inclusion and social and economic creativity.

With Web 2.0, there is a deep transformation occurring wherein the Web has become a truly participatory media; instead of going on the Web to read static content, we can more easily create and share our own ideas and creations. The rise of what has been alternately referred to as consumer- or user-generated media (content) has been hailed as being truly groundbreaking in nature. Blogging and social networking with the facility of user-generated content has created revolutionary new social media that characterize Web 2.0 as the newest phase of the Internet.

New interactive technologies and peer-to-peer architectures have democratized writing and imaging and, thereby, creativity itself, enabling anyone with computer access to become creators of their own digital content. Writers and video makers as 'content creators' are causing a fundamental shift from the age of information to the age of interaction and recreating themselves in the process. Sometimes this contrast is given in terms of a distinction between 'industrial media,' 'broadcast' or 'mass' media, which is highly centralized, hierarchical and vertical based on one-to-many logic, versus social media, which is decentralized (without a central server), nonhierarchical or peer governed and horizontal based on many-to-many interaction.

Forms of industrial mass media, including books, newspapers, radio, television, film and video broadcast media, were designed to reach large audiences within the industrializing nation-state. The major disadvantage of this media form is the criticism of manipulation, bias and ideology that comes with a one-to-many dissemination, its commodification of information and its corporate method of production and distribution (Thompson, 1995). Mass media communication is a one-way transmission model where the audience is reduced to a passive consumer of programmed information which is suited to mass audiences. Both industrial and social media provide the scalable means for reaching global audiences. The means of production for industrial media are typically owned privately or by the state and require specialized technical expertise to produce and payment to access. Social media, by contrast, is based on the Internet as platform and tend to be available free or at little cost, requiring little or no technical operating knowledge. There are also profound differences in production and consumption processes, in the immediacy of the two types of media and in the levels and means of participation and reception.

Even so it is not a question of straightforward replacement. Many of the industrial media are rapidly adopting aspects of social media to develop more interactive capacity. CNN, for instance, has introduced its blogs with viewer participation and interaction and encourages viewers to follow stories on Twitter and Facebook. This means that new media will not simply replace old media but rather will learn to interact with it in a complex relationship Bolter and Grusin (2001) called 'remediation' and Henry Jenkins (2006) called 'convergence culture.' Jenkins (2006) argued that convergence culture is not primarily a technological revolution but is more a cultural shift, dependent on the active participation of the consumers working in a social dynamic. Douglas Kellner and George Kim (2009) theorized YouTube as the cutting edge of information and communications technology (ICT) and characterized it as a dialogical learning community and for learning-by-doing, learning as communication, learning through reflection on the environment, learning as self-fulfillment and empowerment and learning for agency and social change.

The socially networked universe has changed the material conditions for the formation, circulation and utilization of knowledge. 'Learning' has been transformed from its formal mode under the industrial economy, structured through class, gender and age to an informal and ubiquitous mode of learning 'anywhere, anytime' in the information and media-based economy. Increasingly, the emphasis falls on the 'learning economy,' improving learning systems and networks, and the acquisition of new media literacies. These mega-trends signal changes in both the production and consumption of symbolic goods and their situated contexts of use. The new media logics accent the 'learner's' *coproduction* and the active production of meaning in a variety of networked public and private spaces, where knowledge and learning emerge as new principles of social stratification, social mobility and identity formation.

New media technologies not only diminish the effect of distance but they also thereby conflate the local and the global, the private and the public, 'work' and 'home.' They spatialize knowledge systems. Digitalization of learning systems increases the speed, circulation and exchange of knowledge highlighting the importance of digital representations of all symbolic and cultural resources, digital cultural archives, and new literacies and models of text management, distribution and generation. At the same time, the radical concordances of image, text and sound and the development of global information/knowledge infrastructures have created new learning opportunities while encouraging the emergence of a global media network linked with a global communications network together with the emergence of global Euro-American consumer culture and the rise of global edutainment media conglomerates. In the media economy the political economy of ownership becomes central; who owns and designs learning systems becomes a question of paramount political and philosophical significance.

New models of flexible learning nest within new technologies that are part of wider historical emerging technocapitalist systems that promote greater interconnectivity and encompass all of its different modes characterizing communication, from the telegraph (city-to-city), the media (one-to-many), the telephone (one-on-one), the Internet (one-to-one, one-to-all, all-to-one, all-to-all, many-to-many, etc.), the World Wide Web (collective by content but connective by access) and the mobile/cell phone (all the interconnectivity modes afforded by the Web and Internet, plus a body-to-body connection). At the same time, these new affordances seem to provide new opportunities for learning that reflect old social democratic goals concerning equality, access and emancipation that made education central to both liberal and socialist ideals.

Well before the emergence of the Internet and the phenomenon of social networking appeared in the mid-1990s, the model of the 'open university' in the UK was established as technology-based distance education in the 1960s.

The Open University was founded on the idea that communications technology could extend advanced-degree learning to those people who, for a variety of reasons, could not easily attend campus universities. The Open University really began in 1923 when the educationalist J. C. Stobart, while working for the infant BBC, wrote a memo suggesting that the new communications and broadcast media could develop a 'wireless university.' By the early 1960s many different ideas were being proposed, including a 'teleuniversity' that would broadcast lectures, as well as provide correspondence texts and organizing campus visits to local universities. Yet The Open University was not merely an institution that followed from the development of technical mechanisms of openness. From the start the idea of the 'open university' was conceived, in social democratic terms, as a response to the problem of exclusion. Michael Young (Baron Young of Dartington, 1915–2002), the sociologist, activist and politician, who first coined the term and helped found The Open University, wrote the 1945 manifesto for the Labor Party under Clement Attlee and devoted himself to social reform of institutions based on their greater democratization and giving the people a stronger role in their governance.

A Labor Party study group under the chairmanship of Lord Taylor presented a report in March 1963 concerning the continuing exclusion from higher education of the lower income groups, proposing a 'University of the Air' as an experiment for adult education. The Open University was established in Milton Keynes in September 1969 with Professor Walter Perry as its first vice chancellor. It took its first cohort of students in 1970, which began foundation courses in January 1971. Today The Open University has some 180,000 students in the UK (150,000 undergraduate and more than 30,000 postgraduate students), with an additional 25,000 overseas students, making it one of the largest universities in the world. Over 10,000 students attending The Open University have disabilities.

The first and second iterations of university openness have provided significant benefits to society. The social democratic character of openness promoted inclusion and opportunity for a wider range of people than who would have been traditionally enrolled in university. Knowledge exclusivity was challenged by the institutional assertion that knowledge is a public good. The second form of openness, with its confluence of freedom of information and technological affordances, further provided a freedom to use, share and improve knowledge. However, both of these forms of openness are necessarily restricted: the first by technical infrastructure limitations and the latter by resource imbalances and the exclusivity necessary to intellectual property.

The next version of openness, what I call the 'intellectual commons,' combines aspects of the two earlier forms to maximize their respective benefits, while reducing limitations. In this model of openness, the nation-state places education at the center of society and human rights. In this sense, it shares similarities to the form of openness based on social democratic goals. At the same time, it also shares with the new form of openness a culture of social, ICT-driven knowledge sharing and innovation. However, the 'intellectual commons' differs because its ideological foundation is not social democratic, nor that of liberal political economy. Instead, it is based on what can be called 'radical openness' and a logic that provides the basis for protecting and expanding public education and for redesigning the public sphere. This is what I have described in terms of a concept of 'creative labor' that conceptually and in practice pits itself against human capital theory (Peters, 2013).[3]

The intellectual commons provides an alternative to the currently dominant 'knowledge capitalism.' Whereas knowledge capitalism focuses on the economics of knowledge, emphasizing human capital development, intellectual property regimes and efficiency and profit maximization, the intellectual commons shifts emphasis toward recognition that knowledge and its value are ultimately rooted in social relations, a kind of knowledge socialism that promotes the sociality of knowledge by providing mechanisms for a truly free exchange of ideas. Unlike knowledge capitalism, which relies on exclusivity—and thus scarcity—to drive innovation, the intellectual commons alternative recognizes that exclusivity can also greatly limit innovation possibilities. Hence, rather than relying on the market to serve as a catalyst for knowledge creation, knowledge socialism marshals the financial and administrative resources of the nation-state to advance knowledge for the public good.

Consequently, the university, as a key locus of knowledge creation, becomes the mechanism of multiple forms of innovation, not merely in areas with obviously direct economic returns (such as technoscience) but also in those areas (such as information literacy) that facilitate indirect benefits not merely beholden to concern for short-term market gains. Positioning the university in this way might seem overly idealistic, perhaps even disconnected from the tremendous financial realities facing universities, and higher education in general, in much of the world. Reactions of this sort, however, rely on the assumption that the current neoliberal model of higher education, with primacy placed on selling educational 'products' to 'consumers,' is the best remedy to diminishing funding. Furthermore, although individual economic actors maximize personal benefits through their consumption choices, these choices frequently do not correspond to broader societal needs. Free exchange of knowledge in higher education, for instance, does more than provide economic returns to individual actors and institutions. It can also maximize the place of universities in the global knowledge-based economy by collective, education-based innovation, based on radical openness and new forms of collaboration (Peters, 2013).

NOTES

1. This chapter is based on an open access editorial for the *Open Review of Educational Research* (volume 1, 2014) that itself was based on an excerpted and edited version of a chapter written with Garett Gietzen and David Ondercin, both PhD students at the time at the University of Illinois (Urbana-Champaign). The chapter is called 'Knowledge Socialism: Intellectual Commons and Openness in the University' (Barnett, 2012).
2. See the Finch report, 'Accessibility, Sustainability, Excellence: How to Expand Access to Research Publications. Report of the Working Group on Expanding Access to Published Research Findings,' at http://www.researchinfonet.org/wp-content/uploads/2012/06/Finch-Group-report-FINAL-VERSION.pdf; the UK Government's 'Government to Open Up Publicly Funded Research,' at https://www.gov.uk/government/news/government-to-open-up-publicly-funded-research; the UK Research Council's (RCUK) 'Policy on Open Access and Supporting Guidance,' at http://www.rcuk.ac.uk/RCUK-prod/assets/documents/documents/RCUKOpen AccessPolicy.pdf. See also the Research Information Network (RIN) report on these and related development at http://www.researchinfonet.org/finch/
3. See the YouTube presentation, 'Radical Openness: Creative Institutions, Creative Labor and the Logic of Public Organizations in Cognitive Capitalism'; keynote by Michael A. Peters (Waikato University, New Zealand) at the conference, 'Organization and the New,' at Philipps-Universität Marburg (Germany), at http://www.youtube.com/watch?v=iZ5zb8gyAr4

REFERENCES

Barnett, R. (Ed.). (2012). *The future university: Ideas and possibilities.* London, UK: Routledge.

Bolter, J. D., & Grusin, R. (2001). *Remediation: Understanding new media.* Cambridge, MA: The MIT Press.

Jenkins, H. (2006). *Convergence culture: Where old and new media collide.* New York, NY: NYU Press.

Kellner, D., & Kim, G. (2009). YouTube, politics and pedagogy. In R. Hammer & D. Kellner (Eds.), *Media/Cultural studies: Critical approaches* (pp. 615–636). New York, NY: Peter Lang.

Peters, M. A. (2006). Higher education, development and the learning economy. *Policy Futures in Education, 4*(3), 279–291.

Peters, M. A. (2013). Radical openness: Creative institutions, creative labor and the logic of public organizations in cognitive capitalism. *Knowledge Cultures, 1*(2), 47–72.

Peters, M. A., & Besley, T. (2006). *Building knowledge cultures: Education and development in the age of knowledge capitalism.* Lanham, MD: Rowman & Littlefield.

Peters, M. A., & Britez, R. (Eds.). (2008). *Open education and education for openness.* Rotterdam, the Netherlands: Sense.

Peters, M. A., & Roberts, P. (2011). *The virtues of openness: Education, science and scholarship in a digital age.* Boulder, CO: Paradigm.

Thompson, J. (1995). *Media and modernity.* London, UK: Polity Press.

CHAPTER THREE

Opening Up Education: Opportunities, Obstacles AND Future Perspectives

PETRA MISSOMELIUS AND THEO HUG

'Opening up education' is an idea that can be found throughout the history of pedagogy. It has been revitalized in the past decade especially in the context of open education (OE) and the open educational resources (OER) movement. Today, a variety of initiatives are aiming to open up education through the use of media technology, on various levels, using digital communications technologies and Creative Commons (CC) licenses as well as massive open online courses (MOOCs).

Understanding information, communication, knowledge and media has become increasingly important in academic discourses and in economic and political debates, not least in the context of UNESCO activities (cf. UNESCO, 2002) but also on a European level. For example, the European Union's (2009) Commission Recommendation on media literacy in the digital environment (cf. European Union, 2009) aims to achieve a more competitive audiovisual and content industry and an inclusive knowledge society, and a number of projects are being undertaken in "Open Education Europa—The Gateway to European Innovative Learning." Consequently, the Digital Agenda as part of the Europe 2020 strategy has followed. This strategy aims at promoting innovation, economic growth and progress by exploring the potential of information and communication technologies (ICTs).

In media theory and in the discourses of pedagogy, educational policy and educational sciences, attention has been paid to the approaches taken to media culture—whether oral, textual, pictorial, numerical or digital—as a kind of cultural environment in which education takes place and has gained significance (cf. Bachmair, 2009; Moser, 2010). Mediated lifeworlds, mobile media, moving cultures (Caron & Caronia, 2007) and the "mobile complex" (Pachler, Bachmair, & Cook, 2010) are discussed in educational sciences, as well. "Competencies which once constituted the core of all education (reading, writing, 'rithmatic) are increasingly at odds with performative and stylistic abilities integral to this new mediatic order." (Leschke & Friesen, 2014, p. 1) Generally, we are facing a body of knowledge and a number of scientific specializations that appear to overtax human capacities. Media technologies are also attempts to contain the information explosion and to help people dealing with bewildering complexity and the uncertainty of information by technological means.

> Encultured media are consequently organic constituents of processes of education and self-formation, and they fulfil this role in two senses: they legitimate themselves by making themselves invisible, at the same time, they serve as the means by which cultural goods are received, understood and reproduced. (Leschke & Friesen 2014, p. 3)

Apart from other modes of legitimation—for example, in terms of media as communicative corrective, democratic necessity, enabling participation generally or media education for democratic participation—and apart from issues of media legislation and legal matters of media use inside and outside of educational institutions, too often, conceptual aspects of mediality, education and educationability (*Bildsamkeit*) remain underestimated in educational discourses generally and also in the context of OE and OER. Accordingly, we are asking this: How is 'education' understood in the OER movement and what effects concerning education in media cultures are to be expected from the newest trends? In this chapter, our intention is to open up the discourse on opening up education in terms of media theory, philosophy of education and metatheoretical considerations.

OE AND OER—CLAIMS, HOPES AND OBSTACLES

For several years there have been discussions about technical media configurations which promise education for all and access to education without any institutional barriers, particularly in terms of MOOCs and OER. A variety of respective initiatives have been developed using digital communication technologies and CC licensing. Today, open educational resources is widely used as an umbrella term for free content initiatives, OER commons, OpenCourseWare (OCW), OER archives, OCW search tools, academic OCW initiatives and similar activities. Definitions are rather pragmatic in this discourse. In a report for the OECD's Centre for Educational Research and Innovation, for example, Jan Hylén summed up a widely used definition, adding to it as follows:

Open Educational Resources are digitised materials offered freely and openly for educators, students and self-learners to use and re-use for teaching, learning and research. To further clarify this, OER is said to include:
- Learning Content: Full courses, courseware, content modules, learning objects, collections and journals.
- Tools: Software to support the development, use, re-use and delivery of learning content including searching and organization of content, content and learning management systems, content development tools, and on-line learning communities.
- Implementation Resources: Intellectual property licenses to promote open publishing of materials, design principles of best practice, and localization of content. (Hylén, 2006, pp. 1–2)

On the whole, MOOCs and OER mark a mode of *opening up educational opportunities* and disengaging them from institutional ties—at the same time (a) creating related infrastructures within institutions and companies and (b) developing institutional features themselves. However, usually the style and claims of these scenarios of education implicitly appeal to a group of persons who have already had some academic education. This is due to the way these offerings originated. But this does not mean that things necessarily need to stay the same.

The dream of the universal library open to everyone is present in the myths of how the Internet was founded. In the media discourse it is directly connected to the reordering of knowledge production and availability brought about by the computer. These ideas—which still influence the dialogue surrounding media and education—suggest that digital media technologies are eminently suited for educational scenarios. Differentiated metatheoretical considerations on OER are more forthcoming than parts of the mainstreaming activities. Having learning material at one's disposal does not necessarily mean that learning processes will be put into effect—independent from time and place.

Notions of 'openness' are constantly evolving in the OER movement, as Yuan, MacNeill, and Kraan (2008) pointed out, for example in the sense of "sharing software source code, re-(using) content and open access to publications" (Hylén, 2006, p. 2). The term 'open' may refer to free availability and accessibility of content, policies of reducing restrictions of all sorts as far as possible, avoidance of (significant) monetary costs for users, guidelines for building communities of use, modes of licensing or standards of interoperability, and so on. Reflections on clear distinctions of the term and its use, factual conditions and general frameworks and explicit or implicit limitations of 'openness' are not hard to find. Most commonly, different meanings coalesce in the OER movement and positive valuations and connotations are, widely, taken for granted.

Similarly, developmental, societal, educational, moral, political, economical and social claims come together for the most part in the OER discourse. Meiszner and Squires (2013) put it succinctly when they wrote the following:

> Our claim is that Open Education provides a road to deeply modernize education to the challenges of tomorrow, to support complex skills and to adapt education better to the demands of a knowledge society. (p. 17)

As to opportunities, there is a wide range of notions referring to promoting innovation in education, preparing for tasks in the 21st century, enabling educational collaboration on regional, national or international levels, fostering the sharing of educational resources and democratising education, using ICT to improve (self-)learning and teaching as well as harnessing human resources, establishing (new) educational standards and business models, even public relations campaigns and successfully establishing marketing and promotional materials. The following can be taken as exemplifying many similar statements:

> Benefit and impact, to the extent that they can be reliably measured at all, are more a function of *how* ICT is deployed than *what* technologies are used. Hopefully, as this knowledge becomes more widespread, it will help educational systems around the world–whatever their current resourcing constraints–to harness ICT over the coming years to improve educational delivery and reduce its cost, rather than creating additional expenses, exacerbating operational complexities and generating new problems. (Butcher, Kanwar, & Uvalić-Trumbić, 2011, p. 31)

Some initiatives are planned as complementary developments in terms of the enrichment and enhancement of existing activities in formal education.[1] On the other hand, Yuan et al. (2008) pointed out that there are initiatives[2] "launched in the hope that online learning environments might constitute an alternative to traditional classroom teaching by promoting greater student-content interaction and by providing students with greater and more frequent feedback on their performance and understanding" (p. 9) At the heart of many such articulations there seems to be thorough dissatisfaction with regard to much of the development and impact of educational policies, strategies and processes. Accordingly, a strong desire for change and transformation in education might act as a driver in the OER movement.

> Perhaps the most significant sign of open education's promise of deep transformation is that it is becoming an essential part of the discourse on education opportunity and change at institutional, national, and international levels. (Iiyoshi & Kumar, 2010, p. 3)

Not least because of strong claims, far-reaching hopes and technological promises, sceptical voices have also been raised. On the one hand, the underestimation of *educational*, pedagogical and didactical issues, terminological fuzziness, conceptual vagueness and a lack of (meta)theoretical foundation and clarification have been criticized (cf. Knox 2013; see also Hug, 2014). Furthermore, affirmative attitudes toward the economization of education and "the new work order" generally, elitist notions of education and cultural imperialism, as well as orientations toward market needs and financial capitalism on the cost of education (*Bildung*) are on the agenda, as well.[3] This is not only about increasing technological investments and simultaneous savings in educational systems or facilitating "re-governmentalization in the name of de-governmentalization of the educational mainstream" (Hug, 2014). It is also about recurring patterns of expectations toward media technologies which can be traced back throughout the history of media in transition (cf. Missomelius, 2014). Last but not least, there are paradoxical aspects on various levels to be considered. Quite often, legal frameworks do not match the concepts of adoption of OER. And how do we know that the OER movement is not promoting half-realized education (*Halbbildung*) and noneducation (*Unbildung*), too (cf. Hug, 2014)?

Some of the negative aspects might be considered as obstacles which can be overcome sooner or later. However, in examining experiences with these new settings for technology-enhanced learning, we can consider important obstacles as being on different levels:

- *Conceptual Level*
  There is a weakness in conceptualizing and theorizing in the OER movement, a certain blurring of concepts and an obliviousness to history. Viable didactical concepts are widely missing and pars pro toto arguments are frequent (e.g., when a special understanding of learning is considered as an 'all-inclusive' concept or as the pinnacle of education).
- *Institutional Level*
  Apart from the legal issues mentioned earlier, there are other relevant media institutional aspects to be considered. Learners' media practices and their everyday media culture run contrary to widespread traditional teaching concepts in schools. Often, there is a disconnect with the way in which learning situations in school are oblivious to different media or even reject them outright. Technology-enhanced learning (TEL) in formal institutions is commonly based on a rigid vertical hierarchy, making a nondisruptive flow of collaboration difficult or impossible for the learners. By comparison, lifelong learning or adult education finds itself in a quite privileged position, since it exhibits conditions which are (potentially) open to these new forms in their orientation toward active learning and self-directed learning methods.
- *Learning Level*
  Learners' motivations and goals for learning are taken for granted. Concepts for support and coaching are missing in many cases.
- *Societal Level*
  Issues of societal, organizational and generational learning are underestimated. The same is true for the selection of target groups, social mobility,

intergenerational education and reasons for reform resistance in educational systems.
- *Economic Level*
  Business models involved remain unclear among users of OE and offer comprehensive explanation of benefits, actual costs for institutions and the forms of (financial, cultural, social, symbolic, informational) capital involved. Reflections on economies of the commons[4] are barely considered in the mainstream of the OER movement.
- *Technological Level*
  Although sympathies for Free Libre Open Source Software (FLOSS) are widespread in the OER movement, proprietary software plays a prominent role. Protection of data privacy is an issue, too, and making use of collections of big data often remains elusive.

There are minor obstacles that can be overcome over time, such as the setting up of a support programme and concepts regarding the learners' situation, but there are also major obstacles that are concerned with the basic idea of OER, such as those at the institutional, conceptual and societal levels.

Ecologies Revisited—Intermediate Deliberations

Although media increasingly play a role in the educational discourse, they are often understood as mere tools or instruments, especially in the context of TEL. This is quite alarming given the relatively long discussion of media education (*Medienbildung*) in which theoretical considerations of media play a role too.

However, as in many other academic fields, media theory offers a widely ramified discourse landscape. Similarities and differences are not always easy to describe, if we analyze claims related to keywords like 'medialization,' 'mediatization,' 'mediation' or 'mediology' (see Figure 3.1).

Mediation
(R. Silverstone 2005)

Medialization
(W. Schulz 2004)

Mediality
(R. Margreiter 1999, S.J. Schmidt 2008)

Mediality, Mediation, Mediazation, Mediatization, Medialization, Mediology — Exemplary Conceptualizations

Mediatization
(G. Sonesson 1997, Krotz 2008)

Mediology
(Debray 1999, et al.)

Mediazation
(B. Thompson 1995)

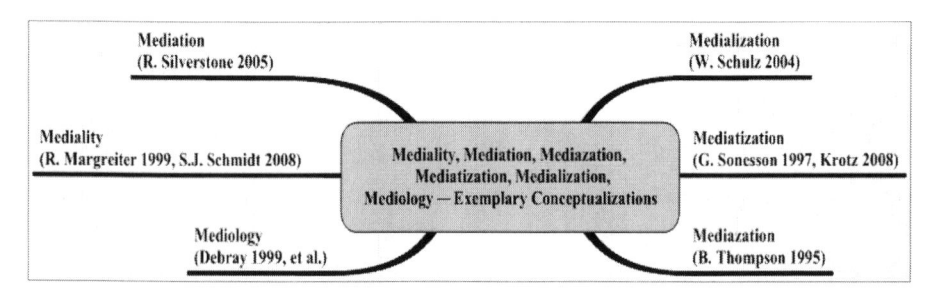

Figure 3.1. Mediality, mediation, mediazation, mediatization, medialization, mediology, etc.

On the whole, there is a shared tendency against isolated forms of taking media as an "add on" on a case-by-case basis—a tendency which can be marked as *mediatic turn* (cf. Hug, 2009). In communications research, considering "the mediation of everything" (Livingstone, 2009) turned out to be a provocative but academically acceptable and fruitful way of rethinking (media) communication.

As to media culture and education, Leschke and Friesen (2014) summarized these thoughts as follows:

> All cultures are interpenetrated and structured by their media.... All cultures are in this sense media-cultures, and it further follows that all forms of involvement with culture, including educational and formative participation, are unavoidably also engagements with its media. Becoming part of a culture, opening up new cultural horizons, and developing and problematizing these further, are all processes that are mediated through media. To be able to reflect on the mediality of cultures can consequently be seen as one of the most elementary forms of reflexive cultural engagement. (p. 1)

Inasmuch as the impacts on education in the context of OER and informational ecosystems are put up for discussion, we want to step back for a moment and encourage some deliberations on understanding both impact and ecologies.

Today, it is presumed that media are involved in the creation of realities and the formation of communicative processes and that they must be considered an agent of socialization and enculturation. In this general sense media are regardad as having quite positive traits, especially when the influences and effects of media are judged as destructive. However, when it comes to how to shape and assess this role, *how* the effects can be specified and to what extent a consideration of media as creating agency or as a socializing agent is adequate, opinions are divided. This is the case for understanding impact or effect, ranges of assumed or actual "virtues" of media (see Figure 3.2) and valuations of them. We think it important to explain related conceptions according to tasks, ranges of claims and theoretical or practical requirements.

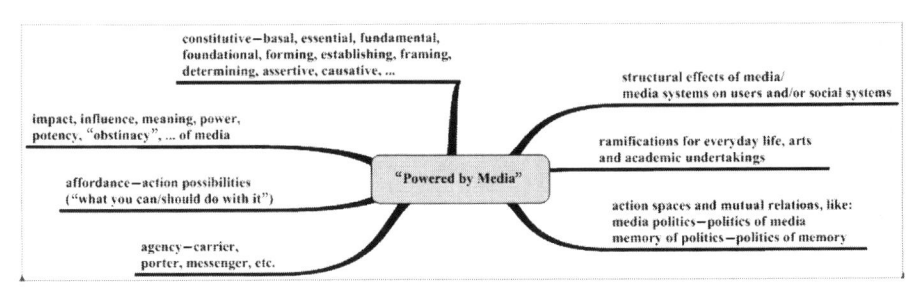

Figure 3.2. By virtue of media: brainstorming.

Similarly, we think that deliberations on conceptions of ecologies and respective compound terms are important to provide descriptions which are as useful as possible and as clear as necessary in a certain context. Even though in many application-related contexts (meta)theoretical considerations are being traded as luxury goods or 'nice to have' items, we think that a certain conceptual accuracy can be very helpful to better understand potential relationships among phenomena and to solve problems.

This concerns, in particular, descriptive and normative aspects. To our knowledge, 'media ecology' was the first compound term in the tradition of the use of the term 'ecology' in pedagogy and educational sciences in the last few decades. It was Neil Postman who introduced the term in the late 1960s, talking of a new predominance of media in public life (cf. Postman, 1985). In his way of thinking, basically, media are seen as socioecological disturbing factors which are to be redressed. In contrast to such a normative approach, Baacke, Sander, and Vollbrecht (1990) developed a socioecological approach, distinguishing four socioecological zones by referring to the ecological systems theory of child development (Bronfenbrenner, 1976). This analytical and descriptive approach is still being developed today in educational sciences, whereas normative thoughts in Postman's tradition are more part of folk theories on media effects and those forms of schooling in which school is considered as 'media resistant polis,' offering more 'stifling' than enlightening 'library air'—as Jeanette Böhme (2006) described it in her book, *School at the End of Book Culture*. Böhme does not despair or simply cancel textual literacy. It is precisely because of "book culture" coming to an end that she sees new possibilities opening up for school, for what she refers to as a new "transmedial school culture."

In media theory, it was Marshall McLuhan (1964) who started working on the idea of media ecologies, which are not to be mixed up with media environments. Together with Kathryn Hutchon and Eric McLuhan, he worked on educational applications of his considerations, too. In *City as Classroom: Understanding Language and Media,* McLuhan, Hutchon, and McLuhan (1977) described concepts for the training of perception, which do not end simply with heightening the student's self-awareness and self-possession, as is the case in various forms of media literacy and critique. Instead, the goal of McLuhan's sensory training is rather the *suspension* of this kind of 'normal' or self-aware experience.

For OER in informational ecosystems, we want to stimulate a discussion of the basic conceptions involved. Although various concepts of information can be considered (cf. Capurro, 1978), it seems clear that approaches of media ecologies, information ecologies, knowledge ecologies (Kuhlen, 2013) or communication ecologies open up different perspectives—foregrounding certain dimensions while others fade into the background.[5] For example, the idea of media ecologies provides a framework for understanding structures and dynamics of media development and the role they play in human affairs. A media ecological perspective assumes that different media technologies engender different mind-sets and ways of thinking: Thus they affect the prerequisites of the educational discourse. This discourse uses the sociocultural term 'ecology' to describe the relation between the learners and their surrounding world, for example the classroom as an ecological system (Rummler, 2014). Although media issues are discussed in school pedagogy and in the theory of education, media theoretical thinking is rarely taken up in these contexts.

At the moment, 'educational media ecologies' (cf. Meister, Hug, & Friesen, 2014) is a rather new term. It focusses especially on mediated learning configurations which attempt to integrate digital media in the media-system of the school and to rethink the educational system, which for ages was based on the values and paradigms of the printed book. Today we live in times of "…a dramatic shift from the linguistic to the visual; from books and book pages to screens and windows. Today's young people are therefore growing up in what has been termed a 'screen culture' (Livingstone, 2002) or within a changing 'media ecology' (Mackey, 2002). The visually represented world is not the same as that represented by writing" (Erixon, 2010, pp. 137–138). It cannot be denied that we are now living in a culture constituted largely by media: They put their stamp on our view of the world and the self, shaping our views of ourselves and the world, as well as our thinking. "What happens in educational discourse when pictures and electronic technology are introduced and the historically dominant textbook, for example, is abandoned in favour of pictorial representation?" (Erixon, 2010, p. 138). What happens in educational discourse—we want to think this through further—when informational sources, modes and practices are changing? Thinking in terms of both information and media ecologies enables answers to these questions, especially as in both cases the focus is not on technology but on relations, contexts, interactive modes and on "human activities that are served by technology" (Nardi & O'Day, 1999, p. 49). "Understanding processes of formation in and through media is dependent on understanding media themselves—their theory, analysis, history, and aesthetics" (Leschke & Friesen, 2014, pp. 1–2). But at the same time,

> the book always retains its place as the medium of choice and reference [in academic institutions]; should this status itself change, then the academy would also have to abandon a wide variety of characteristics on which its legitimacy and recognizability currently relies; and it is clearly not yet prepared to do so (Leschke & Friesen, 2014, p. 4).

Understandings of 'Education' in the OER Movement

Initial discussions of OER were directly linked to the political endeavor of giving access to knowledge in so-called emerging and developing countries. Recent calls for "free educational infrastructures" (Stallman, 2010, p. 155), "enabling universal education" (Caswell Henson, Jensen, and Wiley, 2008) and "Free Education for All"[6] are anything but new in historical terms (cf. Comenius, 1633–1638/1967; Tenorth, 1994). Yet OER debates can be characterized by an obliviousness to history.[7]

In a UNESCO report, OER is defined as follows:

> The recommended definition of Open Educational Resources is: The open provision of educational resources, enabled by information and communication technologies, for consultation, use and adaptation by a community of users for non-commercial purposes. (UNESCO, 2002)

The report is mainly about courseware and educational resources, and it is not about educational processes related to the educational material.

At first sight, the following understandings of 'education' are in common use in the OER discourse today:

- "No specific type"; "any kind of education"[8]
- Professional formation and qualification
- Open access web-based learning and training[9]
- Self-learning

Although John Seely Brown and Richard P. Adler (2008) provided new developments in the sense of social learner perspectives—"This perspective shifts the focus of our attention from the content of a subject to the learning activities and human interactions around which that content is situated" (p. 18)—*educational* considerations play a minor role in the OER movement. Apart from the fact that involving learners as coproducers of teaching and learning materials is anything but new, the lack of pedagogical and didactical as well as educational concepts is not surprising in view of the predominance of economic and technological dimensions. Furthermore, quality assurance is another important issue in the context of educational deliverables in regard to OE and OER (cf. Bergamin & Filk, 2009).

Providing accessibility is seen as the essential activity of the educators offering both OER and MOOCs, while the process of acquiring knowledge with the aid of these materials and communication opportunities is the responsibility of the learners. This practice is found in the history of traditional—yet pedagogically only moderately successful—efforts to use new media productively for a mass audience in educational contexts: Consider educational broadcasts on radio and television (cf. Lehmann, 2013). How the repeatedly propagated social community of learners is supposed to take shape continues to be unclear. The results of initial studies also tend to qualify such euphoric expectations (cf. Mackness, Mak, & Williams, 2010).

From an historical perspective, the OER constellation can also be understood in terms of an "educationalization formula" (*Pädagogisierungsformel*) sense (Veith, 2003, pp. 183–201). Veith (2003) discusses the tension between normative aspects of internal and external legitimation and educational discourses on conceptual clarifications of the core areas and responsibilities of the discipline, while also focussing on the increasingly multifaceted demands of society on the discipline and educational institutions, which can be differentiated by means of educationalization formulas and their historical relevance. In doing so, he provides a helpful historical overview of reproduction problems and educationalization formulas for the German-speaking area (see Table 3.1).

Table 3.1. Reproduction problems and educational formulas (cf. Veith, 2003, p. 185).

Date	Reproduction Crisis	Author/Theory	Educational Formula
1519	Crisis of orientation	Luther	School teaching
	Crisis of stability	Ratke	Didactics
	Teaching (*Unterricht*)		
1648	Crisis of faith	Comenius	Moral education
	Crisis of poverty	Pietism	Vocational education
	Rationality deficit	Early Enlightenment	Usefulness (*Nützlichkeit*)
1740	Crisis of supply	Philanthropism	Usefulness (*Brauchbarkeit*)
	Structural change	Sextro	Industrial education
	Upbringing (*Erziehung*)		
1789	Erosion of solidarity	Pestalozzi	Popular education
	Crisis of legitimacy	Humboldt	Development of self (*Subjektbildung*)
	Foreign rule	Fichte	National education
1815	Restoration	Schleiermacher	Humanistic education
	Value shift	Herbart	Character education
1849	Inequality	Diesterweg	Teacher education
	Class struggle	Herbartians	Ideological education
	Education (*Bildung*)		
1871	Loss of tradition	Progressive education	Spontaneity
	Critique of profession	Meumann	Development
1914	Scarcity of raw materials	Stern	Talent
	Consequences of the war	Humanities	Acquirement of culture

(continues)

Table 3.1. Reproduction problems and educational formulas (cf. Veith, 2003, p. 185).

Date	Reproduction Crisis	Author/Theory	Educational Formula
		Education (*Bildung*)	
1945	New beginning	Pedagogy of the German Democratic Republic	Practical learning
	Rebuilding	Pedagogy of the Federal Republic of Germany	Maturity
1961	Need for innovation	Action pedagogy (*Tätigkeitspädagogik*)	Creativity
	Education calamity (*Bildungsmisere*)	Pedagogy of learning	Capacity to act
1990	Globalization	Competence discourse	Self-organization

So, an additional row in the table could refer to the crisis of neoliberal education policies and an increased emphasis on open and self-directed learning.

However, the normative openness of these learning scenarios refers to legal aspects of use and to technological aspects (cf. Foote, 2005). Here it is, on the one hand, primarily a matter of the compatibility of various resources and systems, although the use of proprietary software or formats has a substantially restricting effect. This is basically the opposite of the idea of sharing, which is why many prefer to use FLOSS. On the other hand, this openness also refers to the licensing framework of educational resources, for instance in the form of the CC. Questions of licensing are especially important for school teachers. What is more, many of the things on offer are also free of charge, so that we can also speak of OER and MOOC participants as having a certain financial freedom—as well as, ideally, being independent of institutions in terms of content and ideology.

As far as the learners are concerned, it is for them to achieve self-empowerment and independence in learning within these scenarios. Typically in the postindustrial West, according to Klaus Krippendorff (2006), there are narratives of free access to information, unlimited contact and the ability to shape the world, including one's own identity. Added to these is the contemporary narrative of opportunities to choose (even though the choices cannot possibly be exhausted, the mere fact that they exist is considered to be a good thing). These mythological narratives are used to channel people's participation in a technological society. Krippendorff identifies these mythologies as being in reality the sources of power driving the narratives. This is intended to overcome the deficiencies of the conventional (public) educational system, while technology-supported, self-determined learning management (private and public) is supposed to lead to innovative thinking. The new, technologically supported opportunities are intended to guarantee an educational programme tailored to the needs of the individual. Free learning materials do allow self-directed usage, but they do not consequently lead to self-directed learning. The characteristics expected of successful learners include motivation, focus and decisiveness. However, the learning scenarios on offer are not accompanied by any support programs (related to the psychology of learning, for instance) to help learners overcome obstructive constellations to meet these expectations. Hence the actual process of learning and the motivation to do so are strongly marked by expectations, yet they do not appear to go beyond the mere formulation of ideals (a "just do it" attitude is assumed). This leaves the impression that what we are dealing with here is less to do with a transformation of the educational system than with a transformation of learners in a subjective learning process (cf. Holzkamp, 1995), who are now expected to make good on their promise in the name of self-empowerment, self-confidence and autonomy.

As Mackness et al. (2010) found in their study of such scenarios, however, many learners have no desire at all for this sort of freedom (and the self-responsibility it entails). Instead, they are confused by the freedom of the open form and expect course structure.

The research found that autonomy, diversity, openness and connectedness/interactivity are characteristics of a MOOC, but they present paradoxes which are difficult to resolve in an online course. The more autonomous, diverse and open the course, and the more connected the learners, the more the potential for their learning to be limited by the lack of structure, support and moderation normally associated with an online course and the more they seek to engage in traditional groups as opposed to an open network. These responses constrain the possibility of having the positive experiences of autonomy, diversity, openness and connectedness/interactivity normally expected of an online network.

In the reality depicted in this study, autonomy is felt to be a lack of needed support. The perception of openness is also multifaceted in that it can even imply an avoidance of networking and sharing. The demands arising from insights of learning theory are handed over entirely to learners by free educational media, while the incentive for learners is found mainly in the focus on personal interest and independence taking place in a culture of sharing (presented in an idealized manner).

Some Reflections on Assessment Criteria

First of all, in view of the manifold of free content initiatives, OER commons, OCW, OER archives, OCW search tools, academic OCW initiatives, and so on, it is rather difficult to provide an overall framework including checklists for evaluation. Of course, there are many options to further develop existing concepts for evaluation and assessment (cf. Chelimsky & Shadish, 1997; see also, Bohnsack & Nentwich-Gesemann, 2010; Keil-Slawik & Kerres, 2003; Schenkel, Tergan, &

Lottmann, 2000) and specify and adapt models, methods and criteria for OE and OER contexts. Undoubtedly, there are special affordances, cases and configurations which require special attention in these contexts.

At this point, we want to further encourage (meta)theoretical considerations and discussions. In doing so, contextual aspects turn out to be relevant. If we do not simply take OE and OER as a hegemonic endeavor or dismiss it as subtle staging of half-realized education (*Halbbildung*) or noneducation (*Unbildung*) and its promotion, the questions remain of which kinds of education and *how* they are fostered in the perspectives of providers, educators, learners, administrators and so on. This requires a context-sensitive approach avoiding the pitfalls of epistemological foundationalism[10] and arbitrary positings. In an epistemological respect, a nonfoundationalist or 'antifoundationalist' approach of the kind proposed by Roel van Goor, Frieda Heyting and Gert-Jan Vreeke (2004) proves promising and useful here (cf. also Heyting, 2001). Although such an undogmatic and non-static orientation accommodates the manifold perspectives and the undecidable character of many questions, it counters premature, oversimplified or arbitrary solution strategies by means of a threefold contextualization of specific problems and topics—reflection on the (a) meaning context, (b) personal context and (c) discourse context (cf. van Goor et al., 2004, p. 176).

In this manner, there is no need to contrast (all-)inclusive concepts (*Inbegriffe*) of education, openness or learning with a variety of deficient ways to understand it. The same is true for articulations regarding the purpose of education as they have been drafted in various contexts.[11] Such contextual analysis would be helpful and revealing with regard to explicit or implicit conceptions of openness, the (background) work of algorithms and the role of proprietary software, as well as FLOSS, and the forms of capital and interests involved, too.

In our view, such an approach can be characterized as relational insofar as definitions and conceptual, theoretical and methodological aspects as well as corresponding objectives, phenomenal domains and practices may be differentiated *and* correlated from multiple perspectives, without encouraging hegemonic tendencies in educational policy or technology, as well as in the politics of scientific discourse or entrepreneurial cultures.

CONCLUSION

Although deliberations discussed in this chapter largely concern academic education, they are nonetheless equally conceivable for certain areas of both professional and extraprofessional postgraduate education. Design, prerequisites and opportunities for using media-supported scenarios within the scope of further areas of adult education, such as basic education, training and educational work with nonacademic target groups (keyword 'education for all'; cf. Hug, 2014), urgently need further research on the part of educational sciences informed by media studies. Educational research with regard to self-directed learning, collaborative and project-related learning and the peer group as coproducers in learning processes, as well as the experiences currently being gathered in distance universities, are but a few of the main thrusts of research in demand in these new contexts—especially if they are not to be co-opted as additional instruments of a neoliberal education sector.

As the chapter reveals, well-founded support for the learning process and, if appropriate, educational coaching, is indispensable if learners are to be enabled to cope with the challenging demands placed on them. In addition, more attention than hitherto must be paid to reflecting on one's own learning processes and becoming better acquainted with learning preferences and personal educational biographies. A change of focus is thus needed away from educational systems toward consideration of individual educational biographies. The changes in the media culture are translating into changes of meaning making and challenge the discourse order of the pedagogies. People today are increasingly cocreative in media production, have basic ideas of media grammars and are dealing with a multitude of dynamic and open media forms: They are engaging in new literacies, picturacy, orality, numeracy and different social practices. This implicit knowledge is widely ignored by education, and the use of OER and media technology in school projects does not change this circumstance at all.

For educational institutions and informal learning contexts, the question remains whether "open educational resources will in future define a *sui generis* **(media) pedagogical standard of education**" (Bergamin & Filk, 2009, p. 11) and also the question how self-directed education and group learning, as well as personalized learning in formal, nonformal and possibly informal contexts, are fostered. On the one hand, one could say

> that *Bildung* could be seen as being supported by OER to achieve its goals of characteristics such as self-determination, maturity, and autonomy. One could also say that OER can offer much support for the positive social and personal vision of *Bildung*. And as a result of individual (and also collective) progress toward these goals, existing resources could be developed and refined, and new resources created—in a relationship of reciprocal interaction and benefit that might even be reminiscent of idealist notions of dialectical development. (Deimann, 2013, p. 193)

On the other hand, in a sceptical appraisal it could be pointed out that there will be hegemonic tendencies, for example, in the sense that OER facilitates regovernmentalization in the name of de-governmentalization of the educational mainstream. Others may ponder issues of consumer cultures "in which everything may be consumed for free" (Bergamin & Filk, 2009, p. 26) or problematic consequences of the euphoric promotion of half-realized education (*Halbbildung*) or noneducation (*Unbildung*).

Potential for various OE and OER developments is there, and respective positive or negative scenarios could be sketched out on the basis of the considerations in this chapter. Further empirical and theoretical research will show which forms of education are taking place and how they have been promoted by the OER movement. So far, developments could be said to have the characteristics of a tightrope walk (*Gratwanderung*), with some media theoretically informing prospects for educational and epistemological transformation in mediated lifeworlds, but there are also the risks of falling into traps of empty technological promises or disenchantments based on overdrawn media expectations.

NOTES

1. Cf. policy and intended use of collaboration tools for teaching, conferences and cooperations at iversity (http://un.iversity.org).
2. Cf., for example, Open Learning Initiative (http://www.cmu.edu/oli/) started at Carnegie Mellon University.
3. For a brief unsystematic list of critical aspects of OER, see http://edtechpost.wikispaces.com/Critiques+of+Open+Education+Resources
4. Cf., for example, http://ecommons.eu/
5. For a deeper understanding, both the study of the history of ecological thinking and metaphorical uses of the term—similar, as, for example Krippendorff's (1994) metaphorical analysis of 'communication'—would provide important insights.
6. Cf. http://www.openeducation.net/
7. Until now, little more than cursory references or preliminary accounts (see Peter & Deimann, 2013) have been published.
8. Cf. Abel Caine in Innsbruck at MWB2013, http://medien.uibk.ac.at/mwb2013
9. Cf. http://openeducation.org
10. The problems of classical foundationalism (empiricism, rationalism and transcendentalism) were pointed out more than 40 years ago by Richard Rorty (1979) in *Philosophy and the Mirror of Nature*.
11. Cf. http://purposed.org.uk/ or http://educationforthecrisis.wikispaces.com/

REFERENCES

Baacke, D., Sander, U., & Vollbrecht, R. (1990). *Lebenswelten sind Medienwelten*. Opladen, Germany: Leske + Budrich.

Bachmair, B. (2009). *Medienwissen für Pädagogen. Medienbildung in riskanten Erlebniswelten*. Wiesbaden, Germany: VS Verlag.

Bergamin, P., & Filk, C. (2009). Open educational resource (OER)—Ein didaktischer Kulturwechsel? [Open educational resources (OER)—A change of course in didactics?]. In P. Bergamin &

C. Filk (Eds.), *Offene Bildungsinhalte (OER). Teilen von Wissen oder Gratisbildungskultur? (Open Educational Resources: Sharing Knowledge or Freebie Education?)* (pp. 11–38). Bern, Switzerland: h.e.p.

Böhme, J. (2006). *Schule am Ende der Buchkultur. Medientheoretische Begründungen schulischer Bildungsarchitekturen.* Bad Heilbrunn, Germany: Klinkhardt.

Bohnsack, R., & Nentwich-Gesemann, I. (Eds.). (2010). *Dokumentarische Evaluationsforschung. Theoretische Grundlagen und Beispiele aus der Praxis.* Leverkusen-Opladen, Germany: Budrich.

Bronfenbrenner, U. (1976). *Ökologische Sozialisationsforschung.* Stuttgart, Germany: Klett.

Brown, J. S., & Adler, R. P. (2008). Minds on fire: Open education, the long tail and Learning 2.0. *Educause Review, 43*(1), 16–32.

Butcher, N., Kanwar, A., & Uvalić-Trumbić, S. (Eds.). (2011). A basic guide to open educational resources (OER). *Commonwealth of Learning.* Retrieved from http://unesdoc.unesco.org/images/0021/002158/215804e.pdf

Capurro, R. (1978). *Information. Ein Beitrag zur etymologischen und ideengeschichtlichen Begründung des Informationsbegriffs.* New York, NY: Berlin, Germany: Saur Verlag.

Caron, A. H., & Caronia, L. (2007). *Moving cultures: Mobile communication in everyday life.* Montreal/Quebec, Canada: McGill-Queen's University Press.

Caswell, T., Henson, S., Jensen, M., & Wiley, D. (2008). Open educational resources: Enabling universal education. *International Review of Research in Open and Distance Learning, 9*(1), 1–4. Retrieved from http://www.irrodl.org/index.php/irrodl/article/view/469/1009

Chelimsky, E., & Shadish, W. R. (1997). *Evaluation for the 21st century: A handbook.* Thousand Oaks, CA: Sage Publications.

Comenius, J. A. (1967). *The great didactic [Didactica Magna]. Translated into English and edited with biographical, historical and critical introductions by M. W. Keatinge.* New York, NY: Russell and Russell. (Original work published 1633–1638)

Debray, R. (2000). *Introduction à la médiologie* (Vol. 1). Presses Universitaires de France-PUF (dt. 2003: *Einführung in die Mediologie. Facetten der Medienkultur.* Bern, Germany: Haupt.

Debray, Régis (1999): Jenseits der Bilder. Eine Geschichte der Bildbetrachtung im Abendland, Rodenbach: Avinus.

Deimann, M. (2013). Open education and *Bildung* as kindred spirits. *E-Learning and Digital Media, 10*(2), 190–199.

Erixon, P-O. (2010). Editorial. Educational sciences and a media ecology perspective. *Education Inquiry, 1*(3), 137–142. Retrieved from http://www.education-inquiry.net/index.php/edui/article/viewFile/21938/28686

European Union. (2009). Commission recommendation of 20 August 2009 on media literacy in the digital environment for a more competitive audiovisual and content industry and an inclusive knowledge society (OJ L 227, 29.8.2009, pp. 9–12). Retrieved from http://eur-lex.europa.eu/LexUriServ/LexUriServ.do?uri=CELEX:32009H0625:EN:NOT

Foote, T. (2005 Open Education Conference). Wikipedia. Utah: Open Education Conference. Retrieved from https://web.archive.org/web/20060918044822/http://cosl.usu.edu/media/presentations/opened2005/OpenEd2005-Foote.ppt

Heyting, F. G. (2001). Antifoundationalist foundational research: Analysing discourse on children's rights to decide. In F. G. Heyting, D. Lenzen, & J. White (Eds.), *Methods in the philosophy of education* (pp. 108–124). London, UK: Routledge.

Holzkamp, K. (1995). *Lernen. Subjektwissenschaftliche Grundlegung.* New York, NY: Campus.

Hug, T. (Ed.). (2009). *Mediatic turn—Claims, concepts and discourses/Mediale Wende—Ansprüche, Konzepte und Diskurse.* New York, NY: Peter Lang.

Hug, T. (2014). Education for all revisited: On concepts of sharing in the open educational resources (OER) movement. *Seminar.net—International Journal of Media, Technology & Lifelong Learning, 10*(1), 1–23. Retrieved from http://seminar.net/images/stories/vol10-issue1/Theo_Hug_Education-for-all_Essay.pdf

Hylén, J. (2006). *Open educational resources: Opportunities and challenges.* Retrieved from http://www.oecd.org/edu/ceri/37351085.pdf

Iiyoshi, T., & Kumar, V. M. S. (Eds.). (2010). *Opening up education. The collective advancement of education through open technology, open content, and open knowledge.* Cambridge, MA: The MIT Press.

Keil-Slawik, R., & Kerres, M. (Ed.). (2003). *Wirkungen und Wirksamkeit Neuer Medien in der Bildung.* Münster, Germany: Waxmann.

Knox, J. (2013). Five critiques of the open educational resources movement. *Teaching in Higher Education, 18*(8), 1–12. doi:10.1080/13562517.2013.774354

Krippendorff, K. (1994). Der verschwundene Bote. Metaphern und Modelle der Kommunikation [The disappearing messenger. Metaphors and models of communication]. In K. Merten, S. J. Schmidt, & S. Weischenberg (Eds.), *Die Wirklichkeit der Medien. Eine Einführung in die Kommunikationswissenschaft [The reality of media. An introduction to communication]* (pp. 79–113). Opladen, Germany: Westdeutscher Verlag.

Krippendorff, K. (2006). *The semantic turn.* Boca Raton, FL: Taylor & Francis/CRC Press.

Krotz, F. (2008). Media connectivity: Concepts, conditions, and consequences. In A. Hepp, F. Krotz & S. Moores (Eds.), *Network, Connectivity and Flow: Key concepts for Media and Cultural Studies.* New York: Hampton Press.

Kuhlen, R. (2013). A 6 Wissensökologie Wissen und Information als Commons (Gemeingüter). In R. Kuhlen, W. Semar, & D. Strauch (Eds.), *Grundlagen der praktischen Information und Dokumentation. Handbuch zur Einführung in die Informationswissenschaft und -praxis* (pp. 68–85). Berlin, Boston: De Gruyter Saur.

Lehmann, B. (2013). Es liegt was in der Luft. Educational broadcasting. In R. Schulmeister (Ed.), *MOOCs—Massive open online courses. Offene Bildung oder Geschäftsmodell?* (pp. 257–271). Münster, Germany: Waxmann.

Leschke, R., & Friesen, N. (2014). Education, media and the end of the book: Some remarks from media theory. In D. M. Meister, T. Hug, & N. Friesen, (Eds.), *Educational media ecologies. MedienPädagogik. Zeitschrift für Theorie und Praxis der Medienbildung* (Special issue no. 24). Retrieved from http://www.medienpaed.com/de/Themenhefte/#24

Livingstone, S. (2002). *Young people and new media.* Thousand Oaks, CA: Sage.

Livingstone, S. (2009). On the mediation of everything: ICA presidential address 2008. *Journal of Communication, 59*(1), 1–18.

Mackey, M. (2002). *Literacies across media: Playing the text.* New York, NY: Routledge Falmer.

Mackness, J., Mak, J. S. F., & Williams, R. (Eds.). (2010). The ideals and reality of participating in a MOOC. *Proceedings of the 7th International Conference on Networked Learning 2010* (pp. 266–275). Lancaster, UK: University of Lancaster.

Margreiter, R. (1999): Realität und Medialität: Zur Philosophie des "Medial Turn." *Medien Journal, 23*(1), 9–18.

McLuhan, M. (1964). *Understanding media: The extensions of man.* New York, NY: Basic Books.

McLuhan, M., Hutchon, K., & McLuhan, E. (1977). *City as classroom: Understanding language and media.* Agincourt, Ontario: Book Society of Canada.

Meister, D., Hug, T., & Friesen, N. (Eds.). (2014). *Educational media ecologies. MedienPädagogik. Zeitschrift für Theorie und Praxis der Medienbildung* (Special issue no. 24). Retrieved from http://www.medienpaed.com/de/Themenhefte/#24

Meiszner, A., & Squires, L. (Eds.). (2013). *Openness and education. Advances in digital education and lifelong learning* (Vol. 1). Cambridge, MA: Emerald.

Missomelius, P. (2014). Bildungserwartungen und Medienkulturen. In P. Missomelius, W. Sützl, T. Hug, P. Grell, & R. Kammerl, (Eds.), *Medien—Wissen—Bildung: Freie Bildungsmedien und Digitale Archive: Media, knowledge & education: Open educational resources and digital archives* (pp. 73–86). Innsbruck, Germany: Innsbruck University Press.

Moser, H. (2010). *Einführung in die Medienpädagogik. Aufwachsen im Medienzeitalter* (5th ed.). Wiesbaden, Germany: VS Verlag.

Nardi, B. A., & O'Day, V. L. (1999). *Information ecologies: Using technology with heart.* Cambridge, MA: The MIT Press.

Pachler, N., Bachmair, B., & Cook, J. (2010). *Mobile learning: Structures, agency, practices.* New York, NY: Springer.

Peter, S., & Deimann, M. (2013). On the role of openness in education: A historical reconstruction. *Open Praxis, 5*(1), 7–14. doi:10.5944/openpraxis.5.1.23. Retrieved from http://www.openpraxis.org/index.php/OpenPraxis/article/view/23/pdf

Postman, N. (1985). *Amusing ourselves to death: Public discourse in the age of show business.* New York, NY: Viking.

Rorty, R. (1979). *Philosophy and the mirror of nature.* Princeton, NJ: Princeton University Press.

Rummler, K. (2014). Foundations of socio-cultural ecology and their consequences for media education and mobile learning in schools. In D. M. Meister, T. Hug, & N. Friesen, (Eds.), *Educational media ecologies. MedienPädagogik. Zeitschrift für Theorie und Praxis der Medienbildung* (Special issue no. 24). Retrieved from http://www.medienpaed.com/de/Themenhefte/#24

Schenkel, P., Tergan, S-O., & Lottmann, A. (Eds.). (2000). *Qualitätsbeurteilung multimedialer Lern- und Informationssysteme.* Nürnberg, Germany: Bildung und Wissen.

Schmidt, S. J. (2008). Media philosophy—A reasonable programme? In H. Hrachovec & A. Pichler (Eds.), *Philosophy of the information society. Proceedings of the 30th International Ludwig Wittgenstein Symposium* (Vol. 2, pp. 89–105). Kirchberg am Wechsel, Austria: Ontos.

Schulz, W. (2004). "Medialisierung." Eine medientheoretische Rekonstruktion des Begriffs, Beitrag zur Jahrestagung der Deutschen Gesellschaft für Publizistik-und Kommunikationswissenschaft [Reconstructing mediatization as an analytical concept]. *European Journal of Communication, 19*(1), 87–101.

Silverstone, R. (2005). The sociology of mediation and communication. In C. J. Calhoun, C. Rojek, & B. S. Turner (Eds.), *The SAGE handbook of sociology* (pp. 188–207). London, UK: SAGE.

Sonesson, G. (1997). The multimediation of the lifeworld. In W. Nöth (Ed.), *Semiotics of the media. Proceedings of an international congress, Kassel, March 1995* (pp. 61–78). Berlin, Germany: Mouton de Gruyter.

Stallman, R. M. (2010). *Free software, free society: Selected essays of Richard M. Stallman* (2nd ed.). Boston, MA: GNU PRESS/Free Software Foundation.

Tenorth, H-E. (1994). *"Alle alles zu lehren." Möglichkeiten und Perspektiven allgemeiner Bildung.* Darmstadt, Germany: Wissenschaftliche Buchgesellschaft.

Thompson, J. B. (1995). *The media and modernity: A social theory of the media.* Cambridge, UK: Polity.

UNESCO. (2002): *Forum on the impact of open courseware for higher education in developing countries: Final report.* Paris, France: Author. Retrieved from http://unesdoc.unesco.org/images/0012/001285/128515e.pdf

van Goor, R., Heyting, F. G., & Vreeke, G-J. (2004). Beyond foundations: Signs of a new normativity in philosophy of education. *Educational Theory, 54*(2), 173–192. doi:10.1111/j.1741-5446.2004.00013.x.

Veith, H. (2003). Lernkultur, Kompetenz, Kompetenzentwicklung und Selbstorganisation. Begriffshistorische Untersuchungen zur gesellschaftlichen und pädagogischen Konstruktion von Erziehungswirklichkeiten in Theorie und Praxis. In Arbeitsgemeinschaft Betriebliche Weiterbildungsforschung e.V./Projekt Qualifikations-Entwicklungs-Management (Eds.): *Was kann ich wissen? Theorie und Geschichte von Lernkultur und Kompetenzentwicklung* (QUEM Report, Schriften zur beruflichen Weiterbildung, Issue 8, pp. 179–229). Berlin, Germany. Retrieved from http://www.abwf.de/content/main/publik/report/2003/Report-82.pdf

Yuan, L., MacNeill, S., & Kraan, W. (2008). *Open educational resources—Opportunities and challenges for higher education.* Bolton, UK: Centre for Educational Technology & Interoperability Standards (JISC-CETIS). Retrieved from http://wiki.cetis.ac.uk/images/0/0b/OER_Briefing_Paper.pdf

CHAPTER FOUR

MOOCs, Neoliberalism AND THE Role OF THE University

DAVID SMALL

The massive open online course (MOOC) phenomenon emerged at the end of the first decade of the new century in a world that was being radically transformed in two major ways. Technological change, particularly with respect to digital communication, was progressing and being globally disseminated at a breakneck pace. No less dramatically, neoliberal globalization had been on the ascendency for three decades, relentlessly applying itself to and transforming virtually every country in the world.

Widely contested but unrivalled by a viable alternative, neoliberalism exerted its influence at every level: at the microlevel detail of the thoughts, actions and feelings of individuals; through the operational processes and systems of the institutions with which they have dealings; and up to the macrolevel, shaping the architecture of regional and global agreements on finance and trade. Among those institutions to be restructured along neoliberal lines was the university.

Compared to its previous incarnation, the neoliberal university was expected to meet different needs of a different society in different ways. Neoliberal policies placed public universities under intolerable strain, providing the imperatives for reform that an emerging class of university managers embraced and implemented.

Constraints on public spending led to universities devising ways to intensify the exploitation of the academic workforce and shunting an ever-increasing burden of debt onto the shoulders of students. In this unsustainable context,

MOOCs promised to be a game changer, a way that people's higher education needs could be met without an intolerable cost burden having to be borne by the state or the students. Could MOOCs represent a new form of university education that would be both financially sustainable and widely accessible? Could MOOCs really mean "free education for everyone"?[1] Does this mean that, as MOOC evangelist Thomas Friedman predicted, "nothing has more potential to lift more people out of poverty"?[2]

This chapter examines the idea that MOOCs could enable an opening up of higher education to an extent previously considered impossible since the demise of social democracy. It also considers what negative impacts might accompany this new world of open online mass education. It argues that the arrival of MOOCs cannot be understood or adequately responded to without addressing at a fundamental level the role of the university in society.

THE RISE OF THE NEOLIBERAL UNIVERSITY

Universities have thoroughly elitist roots, stretching back to their medieval origins. It was not until the 20th century, with the social democratic emphasis on and investment in education, that universities and other tertiary education institutions were made accessible to large numbers of people. Throughout the industrialized world and to a significant, though lesser, extent in developing countries, people from families where nobody had previously advanced their education beyond school were enrolling in and graduating from higher education institutions. The egalitarian and meritocratic ideals of social democracy held that people should not be limited in their educational pursuits by their financial means or social origins but be free to pursue their studies to the fullest extent that their ability, effort and ambition would allow.

Through decades of relative economic prosperity, Keynesian economic systems enabled governments to resource the institutional expansion necessary to give effect to this vision. Universities constructed more campuses and employed more staff to conduct research and introduce students to the world of advanced scholarship. Higher education was made available to students through an ever-widening choice of courses and qualifications. Through their lives on campus, students were initiated into the boundless world of the pursuit of knowledge and learning from their structured and unstructured interactions with academic staff and other students.

This social democratic model of education, like the broader social democratic project of which it was a part, was usurped by neoliberalism. Spurred by the inability of Keynesianism to deal with the economic crises of the 1970s and with the backing of powerful political patrons, neoliberalism was presented as both the only solution to the economic crisis and an inherently superior way for human society to be organized. The citizenry would be liberated from the stultifying social democratic hand of state influence shaped by unhelpful and unnatural attachments to collective approaches to social organization and a questionable ideal of minimizing social inequality.[3] In its place, society would be organized according to a more efficient, noninterventionist market model that spoke to the genuine human spirit, which Roberts called "the ontological heart of neoliberalism…a self interested, utility maximizing individual who is expected to make continuous consumer-style choices in a competitive world."[4]

By the end of the century, and despite considerable resistance from many quarters, neoliberalism had gained the ascendency in almost every country and had succeeded in reconfiguring the architecture of globalization: the institutions and agreements that shape the ways countries trade and interact with each other. Within countries, virtually every sector was restructured according to the logic of neoliberalism with the creation of quasimarkets within which corporate agents would operate.

Informed by what Davis called "new institutional economics,"[5] the corporatization formula that was applied to other public domains was also applied to public universities. They were to be managed according to what was viewed as best business practice, including an expectation that they would be geared toward generating an appropriate operating surplus. Typically, changes to university governance structures saw them oriented less toward "representation" and more toward "competence." Invariably, vice chancellors or presidents of the neoliberal university were required to think and behave like corporate CEOs, with responsibility for orchestrating the complex roles and relationships, the networks that "link institutions as well as faculty, administrators, academic professionals and students to the new economy" to sustain and grow their component of what Slaughter and Rhoades termed "academic capitalism."[6]

In line with new public management theory, it became common practice for these CEOs to divide their universities into quasiautonomous management units which would, in turn, comprise more layers of smaller subordinate units. Through a line management system of accountability and reporting, each of these units would be expected to pay its way, with any budget shortfall commonly being seen as an illegitimate and intolerable form of cross-subsidization. Each unit had to stand or fall on its own merits, the ultimate unit being the individual member of academic staff.

In line with other neoliberal restructuring, the neoliberal university was required to reduce its reliance on public funding. By 2008, many public universities in the United States were receiving as little as 10% of their operating funds from state governments.[7] Other revenue streams had to be developed. There was an increased emphasis on generating external research income which comes with its own challenges, including undue influence over the research agenda, restrictions on the public disclosure of findings and even pressure for a say in appointing academic staff.[8] Universities also sought to increase revenue by running businesses and soliciting donations. Ultimately, however, the reductions in public funding had to be met through a combination of cutting costs and increasing student fees.

It was cuts to public funding that created the imperative for universities to reduce their expenses and increase student fees. However, these two strategies advanced the neoliberal project in far more significant ways than simply reducing public expenditure. They were integral to the neoliberal transformation of the university because they fundamentally altered the ways that staff and students engaged with the university.

The introduction of and increase in student fees helped to replace the notion that university education is primarily a public good with one that focuses on the private benefits to the individual student. As Brown argued, "Many of the benefits of university education accrue to private individuals, so criteria of both efficiency and equity are served if students or their families make some contribution toward the costs of obtaining the benefits."[9] This user pays logic is embedded in the neoliberal notion that education is a tradeable commodity.

The creation of a market in higher education that confronts students with ever-increasing tuition fees also has the effect of constructing those students as consumers and investors. The act of having to purchase their education necessitates consideration of what kind of return students might expect from their investment in themselves, even if that return is thought of in purely self-actualizing terms, with no consideration given to obtaining a useable or marketable qualification. The fact that they are paying for their education with money they could have used in some other way has, to a greater or lesser extent, imbued in students of the neoliberal university an entrepreneurial and instrumental attitude toward their studies.

The tendency for students to view their study in this way is magnified by the significant increases in inequality that neoliberalism generates in society. Under neoliberalism, the rewards of success are becoming so much greater and the consequences of failure so much more devastating, resulting in far higher educational stakes under neoliberalism. The cost of participating in this high-stakes endeavour has seen student debt rise to astronomical proportions, estimated to be in excess of $1 trillion in the United States alone, with one in six borrowers in default in 2012, representing $76 billion in nonperforming loans.[10] Student choice of courses and programmes at the neoliberal university reflects the reality that confronts them in the neoliberal world. The choices students make, though circumscribed by neoliberal policy, can then be (mis)interpreted as evidence that they are indeed the self-interested, utility-maximizing consumer for whom the system was designed.

Not surprisingly, students in the neoliberal university preparing to enter a neoliberal society are more likely to choose courses of study that will bring them financial return on their investment. One impact of this has been to reduce student demand for courses and programmes that do not lead directly to professional qualifications. This has seen a downturn in enrolments in the humanities or social sciences and consequent loss of staff. This trend has been so severe that in many state universities, such programmes and the professors who teach them are said to be "threatened with extinction."[11]

The humanities and social sciences are the natural habitat of the social critic. Their destruction weakens, marginalizes, silences and sometimes removes altogether that part of the university from which analysis, scholarship and research critical of neoliberalism and any other project of the rich and powerful would be most likely to emanate. It also reduces the number of students who are inspired, mentored and introduced into the world of critical social awareness and analysis and who view universities as sites for such critical scholarship. The withering away of the arts, therefore, significantly curtails the capacity of universities to hold a critical mirror to society and challenge received wisdom, especially with regard to theories and perspectives that are favoured by the rich and powerful. The loss of these arenas for critical reflection, therefore, imperils academic freedom, in all but the most impoverished conceptions of that term.

The power of the neoliberal project, however, is such that it conceals the politics of this phenomenon. Education becomes "transfigured to act as if embedded in a competitive environment where the laws of economics reign."[12] By establishing quasimarkets like that of higher education, the neoliberal project can be presented as enabling direct democracy to be enacted by way of consumer choice. Nothing as crude as censorship is required, merely the manufacturing of a context in which areas of study are no longer offered because they are no longer wanted by educational consumers.

The pressure to not just increase student fees but also cut costs was an important element of legitimizing the wave of managerialism that swept through the neoliberal university. Fundamental to this was the "imperative that a new relationship be forged between those who managed educational institutions and those who delivered the needed educational products."[13] The new model transformed academics from relatively autonomous professionals into managed and audited employees "governed by central administrators and non-faculty managerial professionals…who are increasingly central players in the academic enterprise."[14]

In addition to redundancies, there was a major casualization of the academic workforce to the extent that by 2010, almost three quarters of the people employed to teach undergraduate courses in American universities were not full-time permanent professors.[15] The managers' mission is to extract more value from the work of academics, a process legitimized by the imperative to maximize the return on the public funds being allocated to universities. Academic work became far more intensely defined, monitored and measured, and systems of incentives and punishments were introduced to ensure that academics focused on the kind and amount of work that their managers deemed to be of most value to the institution. As Peters[16] noted, an essential part of this process has been to reduce the influence of academics in decision making and sideline democratic structures and academic forums, replacing them with executive-directed systems of communication and "consultation."

An important element of excluding academics from decision making is that it positions university staff as responsible simply for performing their prescribed responsibilities to the standard required of them. It is not their role to contemplate much less challenge the aims of the university or the chosen strategies for achieving them. To the extent that they are consulted on such matters, it is not as of right but by grace and favour of management. This is part of a broader neoliberal strategy to lessen the ability of professionals and their associations or unions to influence public debate, particularly in the fields of health and education. This is achieved in part by seeking to depict any oppositional positions adopted by, for example, academics as representing no more than an expression of their vested interest. At the same time, managerial practices are leading academic staff to do just that, to look no further than their own narrow interests. Individualized academic careerism, argued Kaufman, tends to discourage engagement with a community and over time "to actually produce a kind of hyper-pragmatism, a systematic disbelief in the possibility of radical change."[17]

The self-surveillance and self-monitoring that results from constant oversight and audit lessens the need for academics to be controlled through coercion and have, it is argued, "changed academic self-concepts, role concepts and emotions."[18] Gill spoke of "a profession overloaded to breaking point, as a consequence of the underfunded expansion of universities over the last two decades, combined with hyperinflation of what is demanded of academics, and an audit culture that, if it was once treated with skepticism, has now been almost perfectly internalized."[19] Neoliberalism has rendered the academic workforce less inclined and less capable of either resisting it or developing alternatives to it. Heath and Burdon spoke of "the gap between the exhausted and disempowered everyday life of academics… and the levels of energy, time and collaboration required for effective resistance."[20] This positioning of academic staff within the neoliberal university has profound implications for the arrival of MOOCs and the impact they may have on the world of higher education.

MOOCS AND EDUCATION

MOOCs burst onto the scene so dramatically that, just a few years after the 2008 offering by George Siemens and Stephen Downes of what is generally recognized as the first MOOC, *The New York Times* declared 2012 "The Year of the MOOC." Coursera's attraction of a million users of its MOOCs in their first four months was "a faster launching than either Facebook or Twitter."[21] The scalability of companies such as Udacity would, its founder Sebastian Thrun predicted at the time, leave the world with only 10 institutions of higher learning.[22]

The appeal of MOOCs is obvious. To the state, they represent a way of meeting the growing consumer demand for higher education without either massively increasing public spending or loading even more debt onto students and their families. To students, MOOCs represent the prospect of accessing higher education from some of the world's leading universities without having to make a significant financial investment. University management and staff, though differently positioned, were confronted with the imperative of analyzing and adjusting to a sea change in the globalized higher education industry. This required a capacity to sort fact from fiction in a whirlwind of commentary that Greenstein described as "a perfect storm of hype, hyperbole and hysteria."[23] Daniel examined MOOCs according to the "technology hype cycle" in which the "trough of disillusionment" invariably follows the "peak of inflated expectation" and contemplated whether MOOCs would ever emerge in a form that would establish their ongoing impact on higher education.[24]

Already, research on MOOCs has taken some of the shine off their promise. A survey of over 35,000 MOOC users found them to be more male, employed, already educated and older than the average.[25] The other striking feature to emerge quickly was the very low completion rates for MOOCs. These findings were serious enough to force a rethink to the extent that, in 2013, Thrun himself came to express doubts and acknowledged that there were serious flaws in the way Udacity was operating. Reflecting on Udacity's experience, he concluded, "We don't educate people as others wished or as I wished. We have a lousy product."[26] Thrun was deeply troubled that MOOC noncompletion rates were far too high and devoted himself single-mindedly to rectifying this problem, but his efforts were unable to change the drop-off curve.

Experienced distance educators had been raising these kinds of concerns from the outset. Baggaley lamented that MOOCs were "following none of the educational principles upheld for a century…dispensing with pedagogy, lecture rooms, and even teachers in placing the responsibility for learning squarely on the shoulders of the student."[27] This led him to conclude that "all that has really happened is that solid educational principles have been replaced by a mass communication model with very few principles." MOOCs, he subsequently declared "without equivocation," are "a naïve and damaging blip in the educational media's long and carefully grounded history."[28] Ironically, similar quality concerns were raised about distance education made in the pre-MOOC era by prestigious universities that were later to embrace and champion the MOOC model.

Irrespective of whether these technical hurdles confronting MOOCs can be overcome, deeper pedagogical, philosophical and political questions remain. MOOCs are the latest and dominant manifestation of the open courseware (OCW) movement, which first came to prominence in 2001 with the launch of Massachusetts Institute of Technology's OpenCourseWare Project. OCW was making digitized educational resources freely available to anyone with access to a computer and an Internet connection and developing what was seen as a more collaborative educational project than was found in traditional universities. Bonk wrote of the exciting possibilities of OCW in which "the instructional approaches of choice in online environments are more collaborative, problem based, generative, exploratory, and interactive. There is more emphasis on mentoring, coaching, and guiding the learner than in the past."[29] The OCW movement, it was argued, held the transformative potential "to revolutionize how higher education practitioners, scholars and policymakers think about and define democratic forms of access."[30]

However, critics have noted that much of the revolutionary potential of the OCW movement and the MOOCs that turbocharged it is undermined by the thoroughly conservative epistemology on which the project is based. Rhoads et al. argued that the dominant perspectives within OCW promote a positivist view of knowledge, reducing it almost to a notion of information in which "truth is seen as existing within a particular environment or reality, and…students can be tested relative to their ability to regurgitate accurate conceptions of an existing fact-based reality."[31] Irrespective of the interactivity of the OCW's systems of instruction, they leave unaddressed and unproblematized issues, such as how the validity and importance of the knowledge to be transmitted is determined. OCWs also buy into the commodification of knowledge by reducing the relationships in the education process to only two possibilities: "producers and users of information and knowledge."[32] Drawing on Foucault, Rhoads et al. argued that in this Internet world inhabited by content producers and content users, "what gets defined as knowledge or truth…cannot be separated from the ways in which power operates to enable a particular discourse to be advanced."[33]

The OCW movement can therefore be seen to assume an epistemology that is squarely in the realm of what Freire called banking education. The political impact of this conservative epistemology is to stifle the prospect that education will realize its liberatory potential of generating critical consciousness by engaging its participants in a critical action–reflection cycle. The Rhoads et al. analysis of the OCW literature revealed that to the extent there is any consideration of suffering, inequality and marginality linked to class, race, gender or sexual orientation, these factors are presented from a perspective that views them as "largely the consequence of lack of information."[34] This further disengages people from critical and emancipatory forms of education.

What constitutes a critical and emancipatory project in higher education has long been a matter of analysis and contest. At a fundamental level, a commitment to some version of academic freedom would be common to all accounts of what it means to be a university. A more emancipatory model would also include provisions such as those prescribed in statute in New Zealand: An essential element of universities is that "they accept a role as critic and conscience of society."[35] This latter notion moves beyond simply allowing (or even encouraging) a university to pursue knowledge without outside interference. It imposes a positive obligation on the university to confront society on matters to which the university attaches socioethical importance even, or especially if, these are matters to which significant sectors of society would rather not have attention drawn.

Knowledge, Social Media and Higher Education

It is unlikely that these concerns are high in the minds of a generation that has grown up accustomed to the dizzying pace of change in digital communications technology, in the context of a society restructured along neoliberal lines, being schooled by a neoliberal education system, and which is now contemplating its response to the arrival of MOOCs. What this generation has seen emerge as a university has been described by Richards in very bleak terms:

> The adoption of a commercial ethos means that what used to be a community of scholars, staff and students, engaged upon a common intellectual pursuit of intrinsic interest, value and coherence is in danger of being turned into a series of shambolic academic supermarkets in which student "customers" load their trolleys haphazardly from pick 'n' mix shelves with cheap, nasty, flimsy modularized products lacking in intellectual fibre and nourishment.[36]

However, this is a generation that has not known the university of old and is not likely to recognize what Richards sees as the contemporary university's lack of intellectual nourishment. Even if they did, it is doubtful that many would care enough to eschew any advantages they see in it for themselves, any more than they refused music in the convenient MP3 format because it was a hollowed out version of more data-rich formats. This generation has also grown up to enjoy quite different relationships with and understandings of knowledge and ways of acquiring it. Popular conceptions of knowledge are being radically transformed by rapid advances in and ever-expanding access to technology. There is now a default, almost common-sense view that knowledge is Wikipedia and research is Google.

Alongside this is an entrenchment of the expectation that all manner of information from government departments, corporations, community groups and even media and entertainment outlets will be available online at minimal or no cost. Together with the sense that everything is becoming publicly known or knowable, there now appears to be an endless appetite for a greater immediacy to knowing. In 2012, *Time* reported that 10% of all photos ever taken were taken that year.[37] In 2013, "selfie" was named word of the year by the Oxford English Dictionary, and Facebook announced that its users were uploading 350 million photos per day.[38] Literally anything, from the kangaroo court executions of Saddam Hussein and Muammar Gaddafi, to the choking death of an African American on the streets of New York City by a police officer, to personal naked pictures hacked off the cell phones of celebrities, can now be recorded and made instantly available to the entire world.

The exponential expansion of social media is also transforming people from being just consumers of this 'knowledge' to also defining, valuing, producing and trading it. At one level, one might say that this represents an opening up and democratizing of systems of knowledge. However, it is a world where anything goes, where the worth of knowledge is assessed by the number of clicks and likes that items attract from those who encounter them. It is also a world where there is often a minimal contest of ideas. A study of 'the blogosphere' revealed that blogs tend to attract primarily like-minded people, so ideas often flourish because they go largely unchallenged.[39] It is from this world that people will be embarking on their postcompulsory education and deciding whether they will opt for an MOOC, neoliberal subjects "who believe themselves to be both autonomous and free."[40]

Few academics would disagree with Roberts's assessment that in the age of the Internet, the challenge is "not so much gaining access to the information, but finding ways of distinguishing some forms of information from others," and that important "rules of interpretation" are required to "assist with the task of navigating our way through a sea of information."[41] Indeed, most educators in today's world would agree that meeting that challenge is a defining feature of their current mission. There is, however, another equally important challenge that is presented by the potential of MOOCs to radically reduce and concentrate the number and variety of sites where this educational mission can be undertaken.

MOOCs offer students a choice: They can pay money to attend a bricks and mortar university in their vicinity to take a course presented by whatever academic happens to be teaching it; or they can take an online course for free offered by an academic recognized as the world's best in the field, the international rock-star academic. MOOCs offer policy makers a choice: They can continue to pay to employ university staff in university buildings to provide the opportunity for students to attend university; or they can discontinue significant parts of the teaching programme and steer students to free courses available online through MOOCs.

The logic of neoliberalism has hitherto placed only an instrumental value on the university teaching workforce which has been casualized and controlled by a managerial class in response to consumer demand. Where the demand dries up and students decide not to purchase the product, those teaching it are dispensed with. If this logic is maintained in the face of the arrival of MOOCs, even allowing for exaggeration in Thrun's prediction of there being just 10 universities remaining, there is clear potential for large-scale and ongoing student uptake of MOOCs and consequent downsizing and closure of large parts of the university sector on an unprecedented scale.

The task of assessing the merits of that prospect requires one to focus the mind on the fundamental purpose and value of a university to the society of which it is a part. It requires a questioning of what the university has become and might become. Pate spoke of a primary orientation toward "aggregate productivity rather than the virtuous citizen." MOOCs, he argued, are consistent with and supportive of a technicist, consumer orientation to society. Irrespective of the quality of the handful of professors left standing in the aftermath of the MOOC wave, Pate lamented the reduction of voices and forums for critical analysis which represent "the scrutiny of competing ideas" that are necessary for a vibrant democracy. "MOOCs…are likely to wither away the dialogue, diversity and dissent, and replace the discontent with somnambulist disciples."[42]

These sorts of concerns have surfaced in public controversies over MOOCs, such as the exit of a MOOC star, Princeton sociology professor Mitchell Duneier, and the refusal of the San Jose State University's Philosophy Department to teach an edX course developed by another MOOC star, Michael Sandel. The San Jose professors said that it was "far superior" to be engaging their own students and claimed that this was "a process of replacing faculty with cheap online education,"[43] a sentiment echoed by Duneier.

MOOCS, UNIVERSITIES AND THE NEOLIBERAL SOCIETY

According to the prevailing logic of the managerialism that underpins the neoliberal university, education has no claim to special status. This leaves no basis for distinguishing between the replacement of human tellers in a bank with automatic teller machines, for example, and the replacement of large numbers of academic staff teaching face-to-face with a digital connection to courses taught by one or two leading professors. As long as acceptable levels of customer satisfaction are maintained, the savings should be made.

Lost in this line of logic, however, are the consequences to society in hollowing out its academic workforce by treating them simply as cost categories. In a world economy which is inexorably drawn toward advancing growth, productivity and profitability, the human race is facing unprecedented challenges: persistent and often widening inequalities and experiences of injustice along class, racial and gender lines; seemingly inescapable cycles of military attack and reprisal taking ever more violent and extreme forms; the risk of global spread of increasingly virulent diseases; and the ecological threat to the very continuation of life on the planet. These are some of the serious and complex matters whose solutions, while they may include technical dimensions, necessarily require understandings of and engagement with matters social, historical, political, economic, cultural and philosophical, at levels far superior to anything the human race has yet achieved.

The university has occupied a unique role in promoting and carrying out the unencumbered pursuit of knowledge, advances that are motivated by factors such as intellectual curiosity and social responsibility whether or not any financial benefit may accrue. The positive obligation for universities in New Zealand to act as "critic and conscience" was inserted into statute at the time that the power of neoliberalism to thoroughly transform the university was becoming apparent. The Education Act included a definition of academic freedom as "the freedom of academic staff and students, within the law, to question and test received wisdom, to put forward new ideas and to state controversial or unpopular opinions." It was an articulation of what legislators wanted to ensure was not lost in the rush toward realizing the neoliberal vision. It remains as a reminder of a core element of what a university needs to contribute to society, beyond its coursework and research. At the heart of this mission are academic staff who still in the main want to see themselves as charged with not only engaging in this mission themselves but also initiating future generations into it.

If the educational mission of universities is reduced to the efficient transfer of existing knowledge in identical packages as is promised by MOOCs, communities and societies at a local and national level will lose a unique and essential part of their social fabric. This danger is further magnified in societies that are already positioned primarily as the consumers and not the producers of knowledge and not only out of concerns about intellectual neocolonialism. "By promoting centralized knowledge production," argued Lane and Kinser, "MOOCs limit the spillover effects that can help build the academic infrastructure of developing nations."[44]

One of the challenges of the temptation presented by MOOCs is that any academic resistance to it, as is always the case when people oppose such market forces, is likely to be depicted as simply self-serving attempts to preserve privilege.[45] The challenge presented by MOOCs is one that requires the engagement of society on fundamental questions about the purpose of education, a process that requires critical scrutiny of currently prevailing models and ways of thinking.

It will be a hard task in a context where individuals, institutions and society have been neoliberalized.

CONCLUSION

The arrival of MOOCs has irrevocably changed the world of higher education. The terrain is being continuously made and remade by the deliberations and actions of university managers, academic staff, students and policy makers. Were MOOCs to deliver on their promise of providing free and open access to higher education to all of humanity, they would be a profound influence for the good. However, they are impacting in a context where established systems of higher education are embedded within conflicting and overlapping challenges, interests and power dynamics. Whatever potential gains MOOCs may bring, there are many complex risks.

It would be at their peril for policy makers to either expose the university sector for which they are responsible to a sink-or-swim market competition with MOOCs or to reject them outright. If this is the case, a proper response would demand serious deliberation and wide public consultation over how any engagement with MOOCs should occur. This requires a close and considered examination by the communities and societies the universities are supposed to serve as to what roles and functions are required and desired for the university of the future.

NOTES

1. (2014, March 5). The rising power of MOOCs: Free education for everyone. Retrieved from http://edtechreview.in/news/1038-infographic-the-rising-power-of-moocs-free-education-for-everyone
2. Friedman, T. L. (2013, January 26). Revolution hits the universities. *The New York Times*. Retrieved from http://www.nytimes.com/2013/01/27/opinion/sunday/friedman-revolution-hits-the-universities.html
3. Tooley, J. (1996). *Education without the State* (pp. 54–55). London, UK: Institute of Economic Affairs.
4. Roberts, P. (2013). Academic dystopia: Knowledge, performativity and tertiary education. *Review of Education, Pedagogy and Cultural Studies, 35*(1), 40.
5. Davis, G. (1997). Implications, consequences and futures. In G. Davis, B. Sullivan, & A. Yeatman (Eds.), *The new contractualism?* (p. 228). Melbourne, Australia: Macmillan.
6. Slaughter, S., & Rhoades, G. (2004). *Academic capitalism and the new economy. Markets, state and higher education* (p. 15). Baltimore, MD: John Hopkins University Press.
7. Mohrman, K., Ma, W., & Baker, D. (2008). The research university in transition: The emerging global model. *Higher Education Policy, 21*(1), 21.

8. Retrieved from http://www.theguardian.com/world/2014/sep/12/koch-brothers-sought-say-academic-hiring-university-donation
9. Brown, R. (2011). The impact of markets. In R. Brown (Ed.), *Higher education and the market* (p. 21). London, UK: Routledge.
10. Retrieved from http://www.nytimes.com/2012/09/29/education/report-shows-more-borrows-defaulting-on-student-loans.html?_r=0
11. Munch, R. (2014). *Academic capitalism: Universities in the global struggle for excellence* (p. 43). Hoboken, NJ: Taylor & Francis.
12. Shamir, R. (2008). The age of responsibilization: On market-embedded morality. *Economy and Society, 7*(1), 1.
13. Ward, S. C. (2012). *Neoliberalism and the global restructuring of knowledge and education* (p. 8). London, UK: Routledge.
14. Slaughter, S., & Rhoades, G. (2004), p. 10.
15. Greyser, N., & Weiss, M. (2012). Introduction: Left intellectuals and the neoliberal university. *American Quarterly, 64*(4), 789.
16. Peters, M. (2013). Managerialism and the neoliberal university: Prospects for new forms of "open management" in higher education. *Contemporary Readings in Law and Social Justice, 5*(1), 13.
17. Kaufman, M. (2012). A politics of encounter: Knowledge and organizing in common. *American Quarterly, 64*(4), 824.
18. Heath, M., & Burdon, P. D. (2013). Academic resistance to the neoliberal university. *Legal Education Review, 23*(1–2), 385.
19. Gill, R. (2009). Breaking the silence: The hidden injuries of neo-liberal academia. In R. Flood & R. Gill (Eds.), *Secrecy and silence in the research process: Feminist reflections* (pp. 228–245). London: Routledge.
20. Heath, M., & Burdon, P. D. (2013). Academic resistance to the neoliberal university. *Legal Education Review, 23*(1–2), 392.
21. Lewin, T. (2013, January 6). Retrieved from http://www.nytimes.com/2013/01/07/education/massive-open-online-courses-prove-popular-if-not-lucrative-yet.html
22. Retrieved from http://uchicagogate.com/2014/01/28/years-after-mooc/
23. Greenstein, G. (2013, July 1). Innovation exhaustion and a path to moving forward. Retrieved from https://www.insidehighered.com/views/2013/07/01/essay-need-focus-higher-ed-reforms-right-goals-not-just-quick-change
24. Daniel, J. (June 16th–19th, 2013). *MOOCs: What lies beyond the trough of disillusionment?* Paper presented at the LINC 2013 conference, MIT, Cambridge, MA. Retrieved from http://linc.mit.edu/linc2013/presentations/LINC2013Daniel.pdf
25. Alcorn, B., Christensen, G., & Emanuel, E. J. (2014, January 4). Who takes MOOCs? For online higher education, the devil is in the data. Retrieved from http://www.newrepublic.com/article/116013/mooc-student-survey-who-enrolls-online-education
26. Chafkin, M. (2013). Udacity's Sebastian Thrun, godfather of free online education, changes course. Retrieved from http://www.fastcompany.com/3021473/udacity-sebastian-thrun-up-hill-climb
27. Baggaley, J. (2013). MOOC rampant. *Distance Education, 34*(3), 369–370.
28. Baggaley, J. (2014). MOOC postscript. *Distance Education, 35*(1), 129.
29. Bonk, C. J. (2009). *The world is open: How web technology is revolutionizing education* (p. 33). San Francisco, CA: Jossey-Bass.

30. Rhoads, R. A, Berdan, J., & Toven-Lindsey, B. (2013). The open courseware movement in higher education: Unmasking power and raising questions about the movement's democratic potential. *Educational Theory, 6*(1), 88.
31. Rhoads et al. (2013), pp. 92–93.
32. Rhoads et al. (2013), p. 97.
33. Rhoads et al. (2013), p. 103.
34. Rhoads et al. (2013), p. 97.
35. See Section 162 (4) (a) (5) of the Education Act 1989, New Zealand.
36. Richards, quoted in Ball, S. J. (2012). Performativity, commodification and commitment: An I-Spy guide to the neoliberal university. *British Journal of Educational Studies, 60*(1), 21.
37. Retrieved from http://time.com/3445111/time-picks-the-top-10-photos-of-2012/
38. Retrieved from http://www.businessinsider.com.au/facebook-350-million-photos-each-day-2013-9
39. Adamic, L., & Glance, N. (2005). The political blogosphere and the 2004 U.S. election: Divided they blog. *Proceedings of the 3rd International Workshop on Link Discovery*. New York, NY: Association for Computing Machinery. Retrieved from http://www.scribd.com/doc/7617566/Adamic-and-Glance-Political-Blogosphere-2004-Election
40. Davies, B., & Bansel, P. (2007). Neoliberalism and education. *International Journal of Qualitative Studies in Education, 20*(3), 254.
41. Roberts, P. (2013), p. 36.
42. Pate, R. (2013). MOOCs and modern democracies. *Contemporary Readings in Law and Social Justice, 5*(2), 45.
43. Retrieved from http://chronicle.com/article/Why-Professors-at-San-Jose/138941/
44. Retrieved from http://chronicle.com/blogs/worldwise/moocs-mass-education-and-the-mcdonaldization-of-higher-education/30536
45. Douglas, R. (1993). *Unfinished business.* Auckland, New Zealand: Random House.

CHAPTER FIVE

Posthuman Openings: Looking Beyond Technology Instrumentalism

JEREMY KNOX

In this chapter I argue that open education is constrained by an underlying adherence to the humanist subject, a framework which separates human beings from technology and establishes them as the exclusive source of intention and agency. I contend that a more productive sense of 'openness' might be gained from the perspectives of critical posthumanism and sociomaterial theory, concepts which challenge the dominance of the humanist subject and point to the distributed agencies of entangled human and non-human relational processes. I begin by discussing the deep-rooted relationship between humanism and education, and show how the burgeoning open education movement is drawing on such principles to justify its position. Much of the promotion of massive open online courses (MOOCs) appears to adopt an overtly humanist discourse, where technology purportedly serves to emancipate participants through self-directed study. I highlight two specific examples of MOOC activity, which provide useful ways of discussing instrumental and sociomaterial approaches to technology: firstly, a video tour of a university campus building and its subsequent discussion, and secondly, the algorithmic processes of the social media service YouTube.

EDUCATION AND HUMANISM

Education and humanism are deeply entangled. While we might understand education as 'the dutiful child of the Enlightenment' (Usher & Edwards, 1994, p. 24), we must also then recognise human beings as 'both the instrument and the end product of education' (Pedersen, 2010, p. 241). In other words, education and humanism co-constitute one another; the principles that we attribute to ourselves as human subjects become the rationales for how we go about educating the next generation, and those practices in turn work to construct and maintain the 'us' of humanism. As Biesta (1998) points out, education can be understood as a set of processes through which students are subjectified by a teacher who is already a subject.

While it would be wrong to conflate humanism with the Enlightenment (Foucault, 1978), we might trace such an entanglement in the work of Immanuel Kant, who, building on the privileging of the Cartesian cogito, was clear about the central role of education in the human condition. In his treatise on education, nurture, discipline, instruction and enculturation are fundamentally necessary to 'counteract man's natural unruliness' (Kant, 2010, p. 12). The appropriate condition of 'Man' thus requires educational intervention, such that 'he' meets 'his appointed end' (Kant, 2010, p. 11), that is, the rational and autonomous humanist subject. Post-Enlightenment Romanticism can be understood to have maintained this predetermined privilege of the human, while also establishing education at the core of its realisation, perhaps most recognisably in Rousseau's influential *Emile or On Education*. Following Lewis and Kahn (2010), we might view this romantic rendition of education as "the teleological unveiling of the inner spirit of the human that leads to a community of consensus, harmony, and beauty" (p. 60). Such notions of human essence can also be identified in the powerful educational psychology of the 20th century, in the rational progress and moral distillation of Maslow's (1943) hierarchy of needs, and in Rogers's (1979) attainment of the inner truth of identity through one's intrinsic 'actualising tendency.'

An in-depth historical analysis of the relationships between humanism and education is impossible here, particularly given the multiple interpretations of both of those terms. The work of Davies (1997) is perhaps most significant in exposing the multiple fabrications of humanism, associated as it is with the 'break with the past' of the Renaissance, the 'return to the source' of ancient Greek culture, as well as the 'unbroken continuity with the present' of modernism (p. 103). Following Fuller (2011), however, we may have to settle for humanism as an ideology defined retrospectively. I suggest *essentialism* (intrinsic and uniquely human qualities), *universalism* (a uniform human condition) and *autonomy* (a natural and necessary self-governance and independence) as three central and interrelated principles of humanism. We can perhaps recognise these ideals as underpinning much in the broad and historic project of education, conceived as a practice of developing an innate human potential for independence and intentional agency.

Open Education and Humanism

The seemingly predominant contemporary ideas of self-development, empowerment and 'student-centred' learning appear equally founded on such humanist principles, and it is perhaps the recent 'open education movement' that has championed these tenets most strikingly. Open education appears to have adopted a blunt and overtly humanist stance as its raison d'être, and its critique of orthodox institutional provision. Open education is advanced on the very idea of a universal humanity in which each individual has the right to an education of self-empowerment and emancipation, something deemed not present in established school and university systems. For the open educationalists, mere 'education' is not *human enough*, for geographic and economic barriers prevent all but the privileged from participating, while conventional teaching methods constrain the self-direction and centrality of the individual learner. The underlying premise of open education is therefore an unquestionable category of 'human being,' classified specifically on the grounds of an innate and autonomous humanity that can only be realised through its practices.

MOOCs have emerged at the forefront of the open education movement, provoking numerous optimistic media accounts (S. Adams, 2012; Friedman, 2013; Lewin, 2012; Marginson, 2012) and an emerging body of peer reviewed research (see Daniel, 2014; Jona & Naid, 2014; Siemens, Irvine, & Code, 2013). The high-profile MOOCs offered by Coursera, edX and Udacity appear to promote their services with overtly humanist terms, assuming a universal population of learners desperate for university education, imbued with innate abilities for self-directed learning that transcend context and culture. Udacity (2013) is explicit about its 'mission' as one premised on education as a 'human right,' while Coursera (2014a) claims 'to empower people with education that will improve their lives, the lives of their families, and the communities they live in.' The MOOC software platform, pioneered at Stanford University, thus reflects a broader Silicon Valley 'solutionism' that views web technology as the ultimate remedy for long-standing social dilemmas (Morozov, 2013). The abundance of images of the globe in MOOC promotion (see Coursera, 2014b; edX, 2012), and visualisations of world maps in related research (see Breslow et al., 2013; Nesterko et al., 2013; Perna et al., 2013), appear to set the agenda fairly clearly as one of global relevance and universal opportunity. Yet despite the claim to such a diverse audience, the vast majority of the platform-based MOOCs associated with Coursera, edX and Udacity deploy standardised pedagogical models, comprised of video lectures as the primary course content and multiple-choice quizzes or peer grading as formal assessment (Rodriguez, 2012, 2013). Such designs assume the ability to self-direct through educational tasks, a model for learning that is emphasised further in the so-called connectivist MOOCs that foreground personal networking as the core activity of open education (Kop, Fournier, & Sui Fai Mak, 2011; Rodriguez, 2012).

Situated outside of formal institutional provision, MOOCs tend to assume a learner that is responsible for his or her own education and who is able to self-direct through course material. The emancipation on offer is therefore a matter of individual responsibility. MOOC pioneer Stephen Downes (2012) claimed:

> One big difference between a MOOC and a traditional course is that a MOOC is completely voluntary. You decide that you want to participate, you decide how to participate, then you participate. If you're not motivated, then you're not in the MOOC.

However, the positive tones of such independence and self-empowerment are underpinned by a commitment to humanist principles of universal autonomy and a project of self-realisation. Importantly, agency is situated entirely within the MOOC learner here, who is supposed to possess the intrinsic capacity to govern his or her involvement. However, such a position disregards the ways MOOC participants might be *constructed* as self-directed learners through the powerful discourses that surround this high-profile educational project, as well as the pervasive materiality of the software platforms and social media that facilitate it. The argument that one is required to be a 'lifelong learner' in contemporary society, often related to the demand for MOOCs (Yuan & Powell, 2013), would seem to undermine the notion that participants simply choose to be involved.

Our understanding of the technology-infused education of the MOOC is significantly constrained by the underlying framework of humanism, and the problem lies precisely in the foundational subject/object divide assumed and maintained by the ideals of essentialism, universalism and autonomy. This dualist ordering of the world is the basis of much of Western philosophy, such that education has taught us a common sense in which 'the world is made up of objects "out-there" that we try to know "in-here" within the knowing subject' (Edwards, 2010, p. 10). We might establish this exclusivity as a product of the Enlightenment, where, as Davies (1997) contends, '"Man" is articulated, now, not by but against religion; not within but apart from "society"; not as a part, even a privileged part, of "nature", but outside it' (pp. 122–123). van der Tuin and Dolphijn (2010) describe this fundamental dualism as negative and hierarchical; the object is subordinated to the subject, and the latter is cast as the exclusive source of intention and agency. It is precisely this ordering that justifies 'uses' and 'social' determinism (Dahlberg, 2004; Kanuka, 2008), situating individual human beings or collective society as the driving force for history and technological change.

It is little wonder then that online education has tended to adopt instrumentalist approaches, where technology is viewed as the transparent and passive means to achieve educational aims (Hamilton & Friesen, 2013). This is where a problematic dualism surfaces once again, because the other prevalent position is essentialism (Hamilton & Friesen, 2013), reflecting a technological determinism (Dahlberg 2004) and occupying an oppositional stance in which the innate characteristics of the technology define and control how they are used. Education's involvement with technology thus seems locked into a binary between a utopic ideal of progressive 'tool' use and a dystopic regime of machine control. Oliver (2011) provides a much more nuanced discussion of the 'soft' determinisms and alternative understandings of the relationships between learning and technology. Nevertheless, educational concerns too often tend to proffer instrumentalism as the only viable choice and with it the foundational exceptionality of the humanist subject, formulated as the exclusive source of agency and positioned to necessarily gain mastery over the tools at his or her disposal. The unfortunate result of this position is that 'good' technology is assumed to be *invisible* technology, seamlessly operating to manifest the intentions of its human users.

Such a position can be detected in calls for the 'human element' in online education, where the video lecture is supposed to work against retention problems in distance provision (Kolowich, 2010). Indeed, the video lecture has become the primary form of content in the large-scale platform-based MOOCs (Rodriguez, 2012, 2013). Remarkably, the streamed video encapsulates the instrumentalist position precisely, offering a transparent window to the eminent professor and the privileged campus lecture hall, yet masking the hugely complex technologies, web software and Internet infrastructures that make the broadcast possible. When one watches a MOOC lecture, it is not the video technology itself one is supposed to acknowledge but the image it produces. Indeed, phenomenological studies have attested to the potency of these video lectures and the sense of intimacy they appear to arouse in their audience (C. Adams, Yin, Madriz, & Mullen, 2014). However, such a position retains an instrumental view of technology, where the video becomes simply the invisible means to achieving the supposed benefits of a face-to-face educational setting, and the material facets of the technology are subordinated to their symbolic qualities: those of human faces, gestures and bodily proximity.

In this way, and more generally, the platform-based MOOCs exemplify a notion of openness as access to information (Knox, 2013), where the software is viewed simply as a tool for gaining admittance to the knowledge of the elite institution. The problem with such a stance is that both the MOOC education on offer and the learners taking part are assumed to remain distinct and continuous. In other words, each has an essence that endures, and the technology merely serves to dissolve the barriers preventing the learners from accessing the content. What this disregards completely is how the MOOC acts to reconstruct both the educational institution and the learning subject. This is a much more productive way, I suggest, of viewing the specificities and complexities of open educational offerings such as the MOOC; however, it requires a theoretical perspective that looks beyond the privileging of the humanist subject as the premise upon which such educational activity takes place.

Critical Posthumanism

Under the umbrella term of *critical posthumanism* (Badmington, 2000; Braidotti, 2013; Hayles, 1999; Wolfe, 2010), I suggest that a number of theoretical resources are emerging with which to avoid the limitations of instrumentalism and surface the complex materialities and contingent relations involved in educational endeavours such as the MOOC. Work in critical posthumanism has offered important deconstructive analyses of humanist frameworks, highlighting their inconsistencies and contradictions yet also eluding the dualist orientations of anti-humanism (Badmington, 2000). As Braidotti (2013) claims, critical posthumanism is 'the historical moment that marks the end of the opposition between Humanism and anti-humanism' (p. 37). Critical posthumanism is thus not a rejection nor a negation of the values espoused by humanism but an opportunity to hold their assumptions to account. Braidotti has questioned the Eurocentrism of humanistic principles, highlighting the 'delusion of grandeur in positing ourselves as the moral guardian of the world and as the motor of human evolution' (Braidotti, 2013, p. 25). This critique of universalism is particularly relevant for the broadcast pedagogy of the MOOC (Morris, 2012), seeming to emanate from select universities to an awaiting global populace. Indeed, open education generally appears rooted in the assumption that '"[w]e" may have different types of bodies, but because reason is a property of the mind...deep down "we" are all the same' (Badmington, 2000, p. 4). Yet this sameness is unreservedly that of the rational Man of the Enlightenment, recast as the motivated and self-directing learner, responsible for his or her own educational emancipation.

Specific to educational research, important work with sociomaterial theory (Fenwick, Edwards, & Sawchuk, 2011; Sorensen, 2009) has been proposed to decentre the humanist subject from its dominant position as both the site and measure of education. Encompassing Actor Network Theory (ANT), complexity theory and spatial theories, the sociomaterial is a general term for a range of approaches which attempt to engage with the agential influence of the non-human (or 'material'), with an analytic focus on how things are produced through co-constitutive relations (Fenwick et al., 2011). The sociomaterial thus proposes a world where an active 'social' is not privileged over a passive 'material' but rather where neither has an essence prior to the processes of relational production. Acknowledging the agency of the material in such processes is posited as a necessary critical move in education, which is dominated by ideas related to 'knowledge production, reflection and cognition' (Postma, 2012, p. 139). The sociomaterial is thus concerned with hybrid entanglements and works against the prevailing dualistic orderings that separate epistemology and ontology, the former tending to be of exclusive concern to education (Edwards, 2010). This non-dualistic concern for non-human matter has emerged in the theories of *new materialism*, which claim that 'forces, energies, and intensities (rather than substances) and complex, even random, process, (rather than simple, predictable states) have become the new currency' (Coole & Frost, 2010, p. 13). In other words, without the foundational dualism imposed by the distinction and privilege of the humanist subject, alternative theoretical possibilities are *opened up* by a 'monist' orientation to the world (van der Tuin & Dolphijn, 2010).

This concern for immanence (van der Tuin & Dolphijn, 2010) is about considering humans to be *part* of the material, rather than being subjects who are *apart* from it (Coole & Frost, 2010), and this raises significant questions about the nature of knowledge that orthodox education has largely avoided. Importantly for this discussion of technology instrumentalism, Barad (2007) asserts that such non-dualistic perspectives mean that 'agency is an enactment, not something that someone or something has' (p. 235). In other words, when we consider human beings to be within the material world, as part of its dynamic co-constitutive relations, the sanctity of the humanist subject appears to be a rather *closed* and restricted way of understanding the complexities of agency and intention. In order to explore open education more fully, we need to move beyond instrumentalist ideas and engage with our own position *within* distributed relations of humans and non-human technologies.

The MOOC as a Window to the Prestigious Campus

The purpose of this chapter is to suggest that an underlying humanist framework limits how we can understand the role of technology in the open education of the MOOC, so much so that elitism and inaccessibility tend to be maintained rather than overcome. A salient example of this might be found in the 'Modern and Contemporary American Poetry' MOOC, from the University of Pennsylvania, first offered on the Coursera platform in 2012. The course, which became known as 'ModPo,' consisted of a reading list of poems accompanied by a series of corresponding videos in which the teaching team discussed and interpreted the work. The course followed a typical platform arrangement, involving video content, a discussion forum, multiple-choice quizzes and peer assessments. The first instance of the course was divided into nine chapters of content, delivered in 10 one-week sections, and comprised of 83 videos, each of which involved a detailed, line by line analysis of a specific poem from the syllabus.

Prominent in this MOOC was the promotion of the Kelly Writers House (KWH), the campus building from which the course was produced. A video tour of the building was posted in the early stages of the MOOC, featuring the course convenor walking through the various rooms and ostensibly intruding the space to the watching audience. This video was posted in a discussion thread entitled 'ModPo video tour of the Kelly Writers House—brand new!,' which ended up comprising 101 posts from 57 different named commenters, four anonymous contributions and 21 replies from teaching staff. Overwhelmingly, the response to the KWH tour video was positive and enthusiastic. The following is a small selection of the comments. In a typically optimistic response, participant Nelly suggested the following:

> This online class has managed to upend the idea that online learning is detached and impersonal. How many online courses give a virtual tour of their space? I don't imagine many. Everyone at the KWH and at ModPo have worked so hard to deliver a course that is enlightening, enjoyable, and surprisingly welcoming for 30,000+ people around the world.

Significant here is the notion that the KWH building is the space of the MOOC itself. Rather than considering the software platform, or the vast networks of Internet infrastructure through which the video is transferred, or indeed the network of students as the 'course' itself, this response defaults to the university campus as the authentic site of education. This instrumentalist view assumes that the open education on offer is somehow 'at' the University of Pennsylvania and that the MOOC is merely an invisible means of access, a position which not only disregards the technology but also denies the commenter a role within the legitimate course space. Further comments in the thread surface some of the tensions around this privileging of the campus.

One participant claimed, 'I'm so inspired and at the same time envious' and further stated, 'Unfortunately, I can't even dream of visiting KWH, I live so far from it.' Here the privileging of the campus provokes resentment, revealing the desire for mobility and the significant barriers that stand in its way. Another concurs with a previous comment, suggesting, 'I agree with [Lucy] about living to [sic] far away, but it can be a virtual home instead.' This appears to acknowledge the online facets of the course; however, the KWH remains the authentic site of education, to which the MOOC is merely 'virtual,' a 'nearly authentic' version. This surfaces the hierarchical orientation that is endorsed throughout much of the thread, where the campus is preserved at the core and the MOOC is positioned as a form of peripheral admittance. Another participant suggested the following:

> I felt like an honoured guest being invited into the home of ModPo with all of the "family" there to greet me. I wish a trip to the East Coast would be possible. I'll have to learn from Emily Dickinson and be content to use my imagination.

Thus, even for those within the United States, the ability to travel appears highly problematic, yet deeply desirable, and significantly an educational experience not met by the video content of the MOOC. In this sense, while promoted as overcoming economic and geographical barriers, the MOOC might be understood to intensify educational immobility and offer only continued sedentarism to the less privileged. This is not to deny that moving, even 'virtually,' can be 'a source of status and power' (Hannam, K., Sheller, M., & Urry, J. 2006, p. 10), only to note that the desire for physical mobility is often not recognised. As Edwards (1994) suggests, distance education has 'paradoxical effects, as it can enable people to be kept "in their place", while at the same time enabling people across great physical distances to be brought together through the use of communications.'

It is important to stress here that it is the reliance on a humanist framework that structures-in this notion of a 'window on the campus,' where the MOOC itself appears beyond consideration, and the focus is entirely on the image made possible by the video broadcast. Notions of 'humanness' predictably emerge in the very same thread, with one contributor stating the following:

> The tour of this house made me realize why the tone of your Mod Po videos seems so genuine. Kelly Writers House is a welcoming place full of genuine faces where the individuals are recognised, but not more important than the poetry. The passion starts at the third floor and goes right though the garden.

The assumption of unadulterated access to individuals is striking here, despite the highly orchestrated arrangement of the tour video and its condition as a pre-recorded artefact. Furthermore, the enthusiasm of the teaching team is notably described as existing exclusively within the limits of the KWH property, emphasising the supposed legitimacy of the campus and the marginalisation of the MOOC itself. This sentiment is reflected in a further comment:

> [T]he way that you and all of your students have gone out of your way to make all of us—in all our multitude—feel welcome and part of the process of learning is one of the most humanising educational experiences I've had in a long time, online or personal.

My inclusion of this comment is not intended to deny the reported experience of this MOOC participant or indeed to call into question the valuable and praiseworthy ModPo course itself; rather it is to highlight the potency of the video medium and its remarkable encapsulation of technology instrumentalism. Rather than simply manifesting something 'human,' one might consider the pre-recorded video tour and its enthusiastic support in the discussion fora to uphold a unidirectional arrangement in which the educational institution is firmly rooted as the hub of a pedagogical broadcast and viewers are subordinated to a role of excluded audience. Such a window to the campus further legitimises the corporate MOOC cause, which trades on the reputation and exclusivity of its elite partner universities, which are necessarily maintained in this orientation. Simultaneously, ModPo 'participants' are produced and maintained as eternal visitors, granted access as passive audience to the video transmission and its images of privileged Ivy League real estate. From this perspective, the MOOC seems to be a technology which sustains, rather than overcomes, exclusiveness and inequality. As Bartlett (2013) contends in the context of the MOOC, '[w]e constantly reencounter this structure, whereby declared radicality in fact simply rehearses the most archaic aspects of what it purports to supersede' (p. 5).

Sociomaterial Spaces

One way to move beyond the problematic view of passive technologies of access is to consider open educational endeavours such as the MOOC in and of themselves, rather than as a means of gaining admittance to something else. Furthermore, a more productive way of approaching 'openness' might be to look beyond the framework of the humanist subject as the bounded source of rational agency and begin to consider our distributed and co-constitutive relations within the digital. The following examples are taken from 'E-learning and Digital Cultures,' a MOOC first offered in January 2013 from the University of Edinburgh (MOOCs@Edinburgh Group, 2013) on the Coursera platform and taught by the author. Known as the EDCMOOC, this five-week course was intended to approach the subject of 'e-learning' through the lens of cultural studies and digital- or cyber-culture. Rather than focussing on the application of technology in education, the EDCMOOC was concerned with exploring the ways that popular culture has shaped our understandings of digital systems, networks and software (Knox, Bayne, Ross, MacLeod, & Sinclair, 2012). The course was divided into two blocks: notions of utopia and dystopia in the use of technology, and ideas related to 'being human' in a digital age. A range of public domain short films and animations were used as the core EDCMOOC content, alongside a selection of open-access articles and academic literature. Participants were asked to respond to this material in personal blogs, the Coursera discussion forum and a variety of social media.

While not claimed to be a superior educational offering to any other MOOC, the EDCMOOC made notable use of multiple web spaces outside of the Coursera platform. As such it might be considered to embrace aspects of the public web that a closed and centralised platform might not, and it was concerned with the 'digitalness' of the course itself, rather than its capacity to replicate a campus arrangement (Knox, 2014a). Both the Coursera platform and the various social media spaces utilised, such as Twitter, Facebook, GooglePlus, WordPress and Blogger, were intended to be very much the focus of critical enquiry, rather than simply the tools of access. While acknowledging that the experiences of participants may have been rather different, the EDCMOOC was designed not to provide admittance to an experience assumed to be located 'at' the University of Edinburgh but rather an event that was distributed and multiple, and whose location was a matter of critical inquiry.

Elsewhere I have discussed how the various algorithms and codes in the social media of the EDCMOOC acted to influence the space of the course, in such a way as to constitute a hybrid sociomaterial arrangement (Knox, 2014b). YouTube provides a salient example of the complexities engendered by algorithmic processes in social media spaces, presenting a web page that can be understood to be constituted through various human and nonhuman procedures. Many of the video resources in the EDCMOOC were YouTube videos, which were embedded within the Coursera platform pages and accessed via hyperlinks that directed participants to the YouTube page itself. The comments within YouTube related to the specific EDCMOOC videos therefore became an important space for course discussion and were populated with considerable student activity (Knox, 2014b). However, the way this YouTube discussion space is produced provides a useful example of the distributed and contingent sociomaterial relations that lie behind social media and thus the workings of the EDCMOOC. The 'relevance' of YouTube comments is determined by a number of factors, including 'the video's creator, popular personalities, engaged discussions about the video, and people in your Google+ Circles' (YouTube, 2013). These various contingencies mean that the inclusion and precise order of comments will differ depending on who is logged in to YouTube, their previous activity, and that of people in their social networks. We might understand the comments to be attributed, not to a single human user or the spread of the YouTube audience, but rather to an irreducible and co-constitutive mix of human and algorithmic agency.

Furthermore, this relational procedure demonstrates how human and nonhuman do not remain distinct in the YouTube comments, but rather co-constitute one another in a hybrid and intra-active (Barard, 2007) arrangement. In other words, what we might consider to be the 'social' dimensions of the dialogue are interrupted and reordered by the algorithm, which is itself conditioned by the activity of humans in the social network. This facet of the EDCMOOC might therefore be more accurately understood as a sociomaterial enactment, in which the discussion space of the course is produced through hybrid, co-constitutive relations of human participants and non-human algorithms. This is a highly significant point for current educational concerns, where the assumptions of 'socially constructed' knowledge appear particularly dominant. If the YouTube dialogue discussed here can be said to be involved at all in producing knowledge, then I suggest it would be hard to justify a position in which algorithms were entirely absent in that production and the discussion simply a 'social' affair.

CONCLUSIONS

> What is at stake here is nothing less than a challenge to some of the most basic assumptions that have underpinned the modern world, including its normative sense of the human and its beliefs about human agency. (Coole & Frost, 2010, p. 4)

The implications of critical posthumanism and the sociomaterial for education are profound and question the very foundations of the discipline and many of the assumptions that underpin the burgeoning open education movement. This chapter does not claim to provide an answer, only to signal the need for continued critical approaches in this area. Given its commitment to increasingly complex and interconnected digital technologies, the open education movement would do well to engage with work that is attempting to make sense of the proliferation of software, code and algorithms in our social lives. Williamson (2014) contends: 'The programmable pedagogies of our softwarized world are highly coded acts that are algorithmically assembled into contemporary collective life, thought, identity, space, publics, and discourse.'

To attempt to mask the swelling influence of code beneath ever more slick interfaces (Edwards & Carmichael, 2012), or indeed the idyllic images of privileged campus real estate, might be interpreted as a form of *closure* within a movement concerned primarily with *openness*. I suggest that such problems can only be approached meaningfully through the critical appraisal of open education's reliance on the rational and autonomous subject of humanism.

REFERENCES

Adams, C., Yin, Y., Madriz, L. F. V., & Mullen, C. S. (2014). A phenomenology of learning large: The tutorial sphere of xMOOC video lectures. *Distance Education, 35*(2), 202–216. doi: 10.1080/01587919.2014.917701.

Adams, S. (2012, July 17). Is Coursera the beginning of the end for traditional higher education? *Forbes*. Retrieved from http://www.forbes.com/sites/susanadams/2012/07/17/is-coursera-the-beginning-of-the-end-for-traditional-higher-education/

Badmington, N. (2000). *Posthumanism*. Basingstoke, UK: Palgrave.

Barad, K. (2007). *Meeting the universe halfway: Quantum physics and the entanglement of matter and meaning*. London, UK: Duke University Press.

Bartlett, A. J. (2013). Innovations in incapacity: Education, technique, subject. *Digital Culture and Education, 5*(1), 2–17. Retrieved from http://www.digitalcultureandeducation.com/cms/wp-content/uploads/2013/06/DCE_1079_Bartlett.pdf

Biesta, G. (1998). Pedagogy without humanism: Foucault and the subject of education. *Interchange, 29*(1), 1–16.

Braidotti, R. (2013). *The posthuman*. Cambridge, UK: Polity Press.

Breslow, L., Pritchard, D. E., DeBoer, J., Stump, G. S., Ho, A. D., & Seaton, D. T. (2013). Studying learning in the worldwide classroom: Research into edX's first MOOC. *Research and Practice in Assessment, 8*(2), 13–25. Retrieved from http://www.rpajournal.com/dev/wp-content/uploads/2013/05/SF2.pdf

Coole, D., & Frost, S. (2010). Introducing the new materialisms. In D. Coole & S. Frost (Eds.), *New materialisms: Ontology, agency and politics* (pp. 1–43). London, UK: Duke University Press.

Coursera. (2014a). Our vision. Retrieved from https://www.coursera.org/about

Coursera. (2014b). Globe visualisation. Retrieved from http://viz.coursera.org/2013-02-20-globe/

Dahlberg, L. (2004). Internet research tracings: Towards non-reductionist methodology [Special issue]. *Journal of Computer Mediated Communication, 9*(3). Retrieved from http://onlinelibrary.wiley.com/doi/10.1111/j.1083-6101.2004.tb00289.x/full

Daniel, J. (2014). Foreword to the special section on massive open online courses MOOCs—Evolution or revolution? *MERLOT Journal of Online Learning and Teaching, 10*(1), 4.

Davies, T. (1997). *Humanism*. London: Routledge.

Downes, S. (2012, March 1). What a MOOC does. *Stephen's Web*. Retrieved from http://www.downes.ca/post/57728

Edwards, R. (1994). From a distance? Globalisation, space-time compression and distance education. *Open Learning: The Journal of Open and Distance Learning, 9*(3), 9–17. Retrieved from http://www.tandfonline.com/doi/abs/10.1080/0268051940090303

Edwards, R. (2010). The end of lifelong learning: A post-human condition? *Studies in the Education of Adults, 42*(1), pp. 5–17.

Edwards, R., & Carmichael, P. (2012). Secret codes: The hidden curriculum of semantic web technologies. *Discourse: Studies in the Cultural Politics of Education, 33*(4), 1–16. Retrieved from http://www.tandfonline.com/doi/abs/10.1080/01596306.2012.692963

edX. (2012, November 19). Revolutionizing education on campuses and worldwide—edX. *YouTube*. Retrieved from http://youtu.be/IlNU60ZKj3I

Fenwick, T., Edwards, R., & Sawchuk, P. (2011). *Emerging approaches to educational research: Tracing the sociomaterial*. Abingdon, UK: Routledge.

Foucault, M. (1978). *What is enlightenment?* Retrieved from http://philosophy.eserver.org/foucault/what-is-enlightenment.html

Friedman, T. L. (2013, January 26). Revolution hits the universities. *The New York Times*. Retrieved from http://www.nytimes.com/2013/01/27/opinion/sunday/friedman-revolution-hits-theuniversities.html

Fuller, S. (2011). *Humanity 2.0: What it means to be human past, present and future*. Basingstoke: Palgrave Macmillan.

Hamilton, E. C., & Friesen, N. (2013). Online education: A science and technology studies perspective. *Canadian Journal of Learning and Technology, 39*(2), n2. Retrieved from http://cjlt.csj.ualberta.ca/index.php/cjlt/article/view/689/363

Hannam, K., Sheller, M., & Urry, J. (2006). Editorial: Mobilities, immobilities and moorings. *Mobilities, 1*(1), 1–22.

Hayles, N. K. (1999). *How we became posthuman: Virtual bodies in cybernetics, literature, and informatics*. Chicago: The University of Chicago Press.

Jona, K., & Naid, S. (2014). MOOCs: Emerging research [Special issue]. *MOOCs: Emerging Research Distance Education 35*(2), 141–144.

Kant, I. (2010). Kant on education. *The Online Library of Liberty*. Retrieved from http://files.libertyfund.org/files/356/Kant_0235_EBk_v6.0.pdf

Kanuka, H. (2008). Understanding e-learning technologies in practice through philosophies in practice. In T. Anderson, ed. *The Theory and Practice of Online Learning*, (pp. 91–118). Edmonton: AU Press.

Knox, J. (2013). The limitations of access alone: Moving towards open processes in education technology. *Open Praxis*, 5(1), 21–29.

Knox, J. (2014a). Digital culture clash: "Massive" education in the e-learning and digital cultures MOOC. *Distance Education*, 35(2), 164–177. Retrieved from http://www.tandfonline.com/doi/abs/10.1080/01587919.2014.917704

Knox, J. (2014b). Active algorithms: Sociomaterial spaces in the e-learning and digital cultures MOOC. *Campus Virtuales*, 3(1), 42–55.

Knox, J., Bayne, S., Ross, J., MacLeod, H., & Sinclair, C. (2012, August 8). MOOC pedagogy: The challenges of developing for Coursera. *Association for Learning Technology (ALT) Online Newsletter*, 28. Retrieved from https://altc.alt.ac.uk/blog/2012/08/mooc-pedagogy-the-challenges-of-developing-for-coursera/

Kolowich, S. (2010). The human element. *Inside Higher Ed*. Retrieved from https://www.insidehighered.com/news/2010/03/29/lms

Kop, R., Fournier, H., & Sui Fai Mak, J. (2011). A pedagogy of abundance or a pedagogy to support human beings? Participant support on massive open online courses. *The International Review of Research in Open and Distance Learning*, 12(7), 74–93.

Lewin, T. (2012, March 4). Instruction for masses knocks down campus walls. *The New York Times*. Retrieved from http://www.nytimes.com/2012/03/05/education/moocs-large-courses-open-to-all-topple-campus-walls.html

Lewis, T. E., & Kahn, R. (2010). *Education out of bounds: Reimagining cultural studies for a posthuman age*. New York, NY: Palgrave Macmillan.

Marginson, S. (2012, August 12). Yes, MOOC is the global higher education game changer. *University World News*. Retrieved from http://www.universityworldnews.com/article.php?story=2012080915084470

Maslow, A. (1943). *A theory of human motivation*. Retrieved from http://psychclassics.yorku.ca/Maslow/motivation.htm

MOOCs@Edinburgh Group. (2013). MOOCs@Edinburgh 2013—Report #1. Retrieved from https://www.era.lib.ed.ac.uk/bitstream/1842/6683/1/Edinburgh_MOOCs_Report2013_no1.pdf

Morozov, E. (2013). *To save everything click here: Technology, solutionism and the urge to fix problems that don't exist*. London, UK: Penguin.

Morris, S. M. (2012, July 26). Broadcast education: A response to Coursera. *Hybrid Pedagogy*. Retrieved from http://www.hybridpedagogy.com/journal/broadcast-education-a-response-to-coursera/

Nesterko, S., Kashin, K., Reich, J., Seaton, D., Han, Q., Chuang, I.,…Ho, A. (2013). *HarvardX Insights*. Retrieved from http://harvardx.harvard.edu/harvardx-insights

Oliver, M. (2011). Technological determinism in educational technology research: Some alternative ways of thinking about the relationship between learning and technology. *Journal of Computer Assisted Learning*, 27(5), 373–384. Retrieved from: http://doi.wiley.com/10.1111/j.1365-2729.2011.00406.x

Pedersen, H. (2010). Is 'the posthuman' educable? On the convergence of educational philosophy, animal studies, and posthumanist theory. *Discourse: Studies in the Cultural Politics of Education*, 31(2), 237–250.

Perna, L., Ruby, A., Boruch, R., Wang, N., Scull, J., Evans, C., & Ahmad, S. (2013). The life cycle of a million MOOC users. *MOOC Research Initiative Conference.* Retrieved from http://www.gse.upenn.edu/pdf/ahead/perna_ruby_boruch_moocs_dec2013.pdf

Postma, D. (2012). Education as sociomaterial critique. *Pedagogy, Culture and Society, 20*(1), 137–156.

Rodriguez, O. (2012). MOOCs and the AI-Stanford like courses: Two successful and distinct course formats for massive open online courses. *European Journal of Open, Distance and E-Learning.* Retrieved from http://www.eurodl.org/?p=current&article=516

Rodriguez, O. (2013). The concept of openness behind c and x-MOOCs (massive open online courses). *Open Praxis, 5*(1), 67–73.

Rogers, C. R. (1979). The foundations of the person-centred approach. *Education, 100,* 96–107.

Siemens, G., Irvine, V., & Code, J. (2013). Guest editors' preface to the special issue on MOOCs: An academic perspective on an emerging technological and social trend. *MERLOT Journal of Online Learning and Teaching, 9*(2), iii–vi.

Sorensen, E. (2009). *The materiality of learning: Technology and knowledge in educational practice.* Cambridge, UK: Cambridge University Press.

Udacity. (2013). About us. Retrieved from https://www.udacity.com/us

Usher, R., & Edwards, R. (1994). *Postmodernism and education: Different voices, different worlds.* London, UK: Routledge.

van der Tuin, I. & Dolphijn, R., 2010. The transversality of new materialism. *Women: A Cultural Review, 21*(2), pp. 153–171. Available at: http://www.tandfonline.com/doi/abs/10.1080/09574042.2010.488377 [Accessed March 12, 2013].

Williamson, B. (2014). Code acts: How computer code configures learning. *DML Central.* Retrieved from http://dmlcentral.net/blog/ben-williamson/code-acts-how-computer-code-configures-learning

Wolfe, C. (2010). *What is posthumanism?* Minneapolis: University of Minnesota Press.

YouTube. (2013, September 24). We hear you: Better commenting coming to YouTube. Retrieved from http://youtube-global.blogspot.co.uk/2013/09/youtubenew-comments.html

Yuan, L., & Powell, S. (2013). *MOOCs and open education: Implications for higher education.* Retrieved from http://publications.cetis.ac.uk/wp-content/uploads/2013/03/MOOCs-and-Open-Education.pdf

CHAPTER SIX

Of Two Contrasting Philosophies That Underpin Openness IN Education AND What That Entails

PETER B. SLOEP AND ROBERT SCHUWER

OPENNESS IN EDUCATION

We are now faced with numerous examples of the use of the word 'open' in the context of education. There are open schools, open universities, open participatory learning infrastructures (OPLI), open courseware (OCW), massive open online courses (MOOCs), open educational resources (OER), open educational practices (OEP) and so on (see, e.g., Atkins, Brown, & Hammond, 2007; Schuwer, van Genuchten, & Hatton, 2015). What these terms at face value seem to share is their reference to the removal of barriers to the access of education. Open universities have relaxed entrance requirements, open courseware and MOOCs allow for free access to courses, as do open educational resources and open educational practices at the levels of materials and practices, respectively, although the kinds of barriers removed and the extent to which they are removed differ widely (Mulder & Jansen, 2015). However, there is more to openness than this *prima facie* characterization in terms of the removal of barriers reveals. A brief overview of some existing definitions of openness in education can help to make this evident.

An early definition was framed in 1975 by Brian Hill in a book devoted to the philosophy of open education (Hill, 1975; Nyberg, 1975). He discerned *procedural*, *normative* and *revolutionary* openness, which in turn refer to attendance, a learner-centered perspective and, in Hill's own words "the availability to oppressed classes of genuine openness in curriculum choices and learning procedures as a means of accelerating cataclysmic social change" (Deimann & Sloep, 2013, p. 4). This threefold characterization is still recognizable, although at present a different wording is chosen and nuance is added. Thus under the heading of *classical* openness, Fred Mulder and Ben Janssen (2013) discerned six dimensions in which learners can take responsibility for their own learning:

- *Freedom of time, pace and place:* Learners can begin a course or programme at any point during the year and study at any time, determine their own pace and study wherever they like.
- *Open access:* Anybody is admitted irrespective of prior education.
- *Open to a wide variety of target groups:* There is no or at least very little prior selection of learners who can be admitted and learners who can't.
- *Open programming:* Learners can mix and match courses at their liking.

This classical openness seems to be a mix of the technical, normative and revolutionary forms of openness of Hill, if we leave out his revolutionary agenda. Sloep and colleagues (2012) and Deimann and Sloep (2013) subsumed freedom of place, pace and time under the heading of *logistic* openness and added *didactic* openness into the mix, which subsumes open programming but also refers to the freedom to choose a didactic arrangement (solitary versus group work, for example) of one's choosing. Another aspect that is absent from Hill's definition is technology, which at present is prominent in education but at the time was virtually absent. Mulder and Janssen (2013) referred to this aspect as *digital* openness, which encompasses a number of forms of openness, *domains* as they called them. Not all of these forms have educational significance except for OERs, which, according to the authors, are modelled after open software code (one of the other domains).

This brief and eclectic overview shows that openness in education comes in various guises. But it also underscores our initial assumption that openness is about the freedom that learners have to take control of their own education, to access education in ways that they themselves see fit. However, we believe that this is not the entire story; indeed, a more trenchant story may be told by focusing on a deeper layer of analysis. To advance on the story we want to tell, we intend to show that such an analysis reveals the existence of two philosophies that result in radically different kinds of openness. These philosophies embrace either a *humanitarian* system of values or a *utilitarian* one. Our claim is that open education is currently at a crossroad: In designing open education, one should consciously and overtly subscribe to either a humanitarian or a utilitarian system of values, lest values that we hold dear may surreptitiously disappear from the open educational table.

An Extremely Short History of Openness in Education

In exploring and defending our thesis, in this section we first succinctly cover the postwar history of openness to better flesh out our main thesis in the next main section. Rather than attempting to straddle the full breadth of all types of educational openness mentioned earlier, we limit ourselves to only two types: *openness in universities* and *openness in MOOCs*. This is done for reasons of manageability, but more importantly, we also believe that these two forms of openness allow us best to tell the story we want to tell. In our final discussion, we briefly go into the justification of this assumption.

There is one more preliminary issue: Openness in universities seems to attach to the institutional level and openness in MOOCs to the level of individual courses. It would therefore seem that by comparing the two, we commit a category mistake. However, we believe this not to be the case. Universities offer programmes through distinct courses, and many of their institutional policies will carry over to these courses. A policy of no entrance requirements, as is characteristic of many open universities, affects the admittance to individual courses. Conversely, MOOCs are individual courses, but they are offered by MOOC providers, which all impose their own rules and regulations on the courses they offer. The comparison we are about to make is grounded in both of these mutually tied levels.

Open Universities

The Open University was founded in Britain in 1969, after a four-year planning period. It was arguably the first genuine open university,[1] in that it had relaxed entrance requirements (Peter & Deimann, 2013). It set the stage for a great many others. To name a haphazard few, Athabasca University in Canada (Alberta) followed a year later in 1970; The Open University of the Netherlands opened its doors for students in 1984, the same year in which the Universitas Terbuka of Indonesia was founded; the Indira Gandhi National Open University of India—according to Wikipedia, the largest open university of the world—was established in 1985; the Hellenic Open University of Greece was founded in 1992; and finally, the Open University of Catalonia began its activities in the academic year 1995–1996.[2] This brief overview, which fails to do justice to the many other initiatives in the world to erect open universities, suffices to establish that the idea of an open university caught on in various places, in Europe but also in the world at large. It seems that open education conceived of as a form of education that seeks to widen access, particularly relative to extant formal higher education systems, was widely embraced in the final decades of the previous century.

Open access is not to be confused with the absence of any monetary charges. Open universities have different arrangements for recovering their operational costs. These may range from being paid for in full out of public funding to no public funding at all, although we are not aware of any examples of the latter. Using the case of The Open University of the Netherlands as an example, about 80% of its operational costs are covered by government funds; the remainder comes out of the enrolment and tuition fees the students pay.[3] Obviously, this requirement to pay for access amounts to erecting an obstacle to access, particularly if the monetary compensation asked is high relative to the average standard of living and no compensation programmes are in place. But it is only one of the many obstacles one may encounter; requirements with respect to prior education is another, perhaps more difficult one to overcome. The presence of compensatory measures, paid for out of public funds or by the student's employer, clearly lowers this barrier to access. So it is still fair to conclude that, by and large, open universities lower the threshold for access to higher education, for obtaining a genuine university degree.

A means of keeping the operational costs of an open university low is the choosing of an appropriate pedagogy. Traditional universities[4] very much rely on a model in which relatively little money is spent in the design phase of a course (design time) and much on the actual deployment ('teaching') of it: the lectures, work groups and so on (run time). In the past, this model was enforced by the lack of appropriate technologies to disseminate information in anything other than large joint sessions (large-scale lectures). And traditional universities by and large still follow this mode. For open universities, however, large-scale lectures was never a genuine option. Perhaps lectures could be televised, but the issue was always that students had little opportunity to interact with their teachers, which significantly detracted from the quality of their learning experiences. So open universities developed a pedagogy which heavily depended on investing in the development of courses and spending as little money as possible on running them. That way too, increases in the numbers of students could be accommodated with little additional cost to the university. Of course, the advent of the Internet, particularly the social web, which allowed for synchronous interaction between teachers and students, removed the old limiting conditions and consequently made open universities rethink their pedagogical commitments. Open universities such as The Open University in the United Kingdom, Athabasca University, and The Open University of the Netherland are in the midst of this transition (Sloep, 2013). But that is another story.

MOOCs

The full history of MOOCs is too immature to be written. It is too early for anyone to distance themselves sufficiently to oversee all relevant and ignore all irrelevant MOOC-related events. Also, MOOC development is still in full swing, with many conferences, journal articles (often in special issues) and projects devoted to its delineation.⁵ This particular section is not to be seen as a contribution to the writing of the definitive MOOC history. It is a mere recount of a number of notable events, particularly those that are relevant in the context of the story we want to tell.⁶

For reasons that will become clear later, we let MOOC history begin with the introductory course in artificial intelligence that Stanford professors Sebastian Thrun and Peter Norvig organised in the autumn of 2011.⁷ The course was mainly intended to serve their residential students, but in an entrepreneurial move, they decided to open it up for free to students anywhere in the world, with baffling results. Approximately 160,000 students from 200 different countries all over the word registered for the class (Rodriguez, 2013). Since then, many more MOOCs were set up, in Stanford, also at MIT and Harvard, and soon all over the world.

Seeded by an influx of venture capital, Thrun was quick to set up a company, Udacity, that provided an online platform for the various MOOCs they intended to host. At about the same time, their Stanford colleagues, Andrew Ng and Daphne Koller, followed with their own company, Coursera. In contrast with Udacity, which created its own content (mainly in science subjects), Coursera's content was provided by 'traditional' universities and their professors, also being helped on its way by venture capital. Universities worldwide could join their platform, where, in an attempt to establish a high quality brand, the company was quite selective about who could and who could not join in.⁸ In 2013, Telefónica of Spain and Banco Santander jointly founded the Miriada X platform, which quickly garnered a huge following in Latin America. In 2014, it already had become the third largest MOOC provider, after Coursera and edX.⁹ The Open University in the United Kingdom founded the FutureLearn consortium, which was launched in September 2013 (Gaebel, 2014). On their heels, several other initiatives followed, some squarely in line with the setup of Udacity and Coursera, others, mainly in continental Europe, such as iversity (2012) and OpenupEd (2013), with slightly different approaches (Gaebel, 2014). On the face of it, these approaches seem to be more in line with that of edX, which grew out of MIT's commitment to OER and OCW.

In MOOCs, courses are free in the sense that no enrolment fee has to be paid, but somehow the universities involved and the MOOC providers need to recoup their investments. There is an ongoing and lengthy discussion about viable MOOC business models. An early volley was launched in July 2013 by *The Economist*.¹⁰ Chrysanthos Dellarocas and Marshall Van Alstyne (2013) conducted a very thorough analysis of MOOC business models. Among the sources of income are fees for acquiring a certificate of attendance and fees for the opportunity to sit in on an exam and be graded.¹¹ Other sources of income are selling student data to anybody with an interest in them, such as recruitment agencies, corporations, universities, and so on.¹² This is very much like the business model of online social services, such as Google, Gmail, Facebook and Twitter, in which the companies that buy the data are the real customers, not the users. Free access is offset by willingly parting with one's data.

We suggest that it is in particular the latter type of income prospects that prompted the involvement of venture capital and large companies. Their authors' argument was probably one of analogy. The first element in the analogy is that companies and even entire industries who fail to judge the power of the Internet appropriately have a hard time surviving unless they innovate. We are referring here to the music, film and most recently book publishing industries. These relied on a business model in which media (CDs, DVDs, paper books) were used to diffuse content; the costs of media reproduction, financially and in terms of time needed, were high, and the quality of every next copy went down significantly as distribution and storage relied on analog technologies. The advent of the Internet, with its reliance on digital distribution means, made media other than hard disks superfluous, made the costs of producing copies negligible and, because of its reliance on digital data, made their quality identical to that of the original. This effectively ruined the viability of the original, business model (which the industries nevertheless tried to uphold). Second, MOOC venture capitalists saw how companies such as Apple (iTunes), Netflix and Amazon managed to take a sizeable share of the music, film and book markets precisely because they better understood the affordances of the Internet (Anderson, 2009). Their argument probably was that, if the education 'industry' is subject to the same logic of the Internet, universities as we know them are bound to disappear and a large market for Internet-based education is for the taking.

This argument assumes a high similarity between the notions of education and content distribution. And indeed, MOOC providers profess to adhere to a pedagogy of mastery learning, that is, assimilating mere content until a standardised test certifies that one indeed has acquired a sufficient level of mastery. Traditional ingredients of such a pedagogy are lectures and sessions, which organise the content for the student in sizeable chunks, arranged in their proper order, with tutors or teaching assistants who help iron out the final misunderstanding. In the MOOC realm, this has been translated into short videos, reading materials and self-tests.

Openness: Two Contrasting Views

Through the free access they provide to pedagogically enriched content, MOOCs no doubt contribute to increasing access to education. However, there is a proviso. One has to pay a modest sum of money to obtain a certificate of participation and more to obtain a certificate of attainment, which requires one to pass a test. However, much more important to note is that neither of these certificates can be used to count toward the fulfilment of a university degree. So MOOCs do not increase access to *higher education* in the sense of a higher education degree. This stands in contrast with open universities, whose purpose is to do precisely that. But there is a proviso here too: Access to a higher education degree comes at a price, the cumulative costs of the individual course modules. This suggests that open universities and MOOCs each fill their own niche in the education ecosystem. If you want a degree, go and study at an open university; if you want to acquire knowledge at a higher education level without necessarily gaining a degree, a MOOC is your best choice. And indeed, research seems to show that MOOCs are increasingly used by people with academic degrees who want to broaden their knowledge or further develop themselves professionally (Falconer, McGill, Littlejohn, & Boursinou, 2013; Grainger, 2013; Garreta-Domingo, Hernández-Leo, Mor, & Sloep, 2015). However, this analysis misses an important point. To see this, we need to look at the wider sociopolitical situation in which open universities and later on MOOCs emerged and further developed.

Decades of Solidarity

On December 10th, 1948, the Universal Declaration of Human Rights[13] was adopted by the United Nations General Assembly. It counts 30 articles, of which Articles 1 and 2 are best known. Article 1 states, "All human beings are born free and equal in dignity and rights." Article 2 states, "Everyone is entitled to all the rights and freedoms set forth in this Declaration." These 2 articles form the foundation on which the other 28 have been built, including Article 26, which is the most important in this context. It contains three clauses, the first of which reads as follows:

> Article 26.1 Everyone has the right to education. Education shall be free, at least in the elementary and fundamental stages. Elementary education shall be compulsory. Technical and professional education shall be made generally available and higher education shall be equally accessible to all on the basis of merit.

Clearly, for the traditional universities, merit was an important factor of their access policies, but it was never the only one. The right prior school, the right skin colour, committed and/or affluent parents were among the factors that were perhaps more decisive than capability alone (Wubbels, 2014). It is safe to say that, although many countries adopted the Universal Declaration, they still had a lot of work ahead of them to meet Article 26.1's requirement to make higher education accessible to all.

That work is extensively discussed in the UNESCO report entitled "Learning to Be," written by Edgar Faure and colleagues (1972). Faure was no doubt influenced by the just-published report of the Club of Rome, "The Limits to Growth" (D. H. Meadows, D. L. Meadows, Randers, & Behrens, 1972), which predicted the end of civilisation as we know it if mankind would not succeed in putting an end to the exponential growth of resource use and population growth. In the preamble to the report, Faure pleads for solidarity in dealing with the challenges of the time. In the final sentences of his preamble, after having established that "the various sectors of human development and social life are inseparable from each other," he sees a solution only forthcoming if we acknowledge that "[t]his age, which has been called that of the finite world, can only be the age of total man: that is to say, man entire and all of man" (Faure et al., 1972, p. xxxix), in short, the age of solidarity.

This sentiment is also echoed in the attitude of the peoples of Europe in the postwar period of the 1950s. It was a period of hard work and sacrifices but also a period of much optimism, of belief in a better world and in mankind's ability to build one (Judt, 2005; Mak, 2004). The adoption of the Universal Declaration of Human Rights indeed testifies to that optimism. Another example thereof constitutes the establishment of the European Union, first as the European Coal and Steel Community in 1952, to be followed by the European Economic Community in 1957, which in its turn through the signing of the treaty of Maastricht in 1992 was succeeded by the current European Union (Judt, 2005; Mak, 2004). The European Union's contribution "to the advancement of peace and reconciliation, democracy, and human rights in Europe" cannot be overestimated, as is underscored by the 2012 Nobel Peace Prize the European Union as a whole received.[14] So there definitely was a willingness to sacrifice but also a keen resolve to exercise solidarity in dealing with Europe's problems.

It is against this backdrop of solidarity that several countries inside and outside of Europe decided to establish open universities.

A Change of Attitude

In 1996, about the time that the last open universities were established, a seminal report was published by the UNESCO International Commission on Education for the Twenty-first Century (Delors, 1996). This commission was headed by Jacques Delors, a well-known European politician who, among other achievements, presided over the European Commission for 10 years (from 1985 to 1995). The report has been highly influential, commensurate to the political clout its chair and members had. The commission obviously built on earlier work, for example, on the ideas put forth in the Faure report already mentioned (Faure et al., 1972) but also on the progressive and humanitarian thoughts of educators and philosophers such as John Dewey, Célestin Freinet, and Paulo Freire (Sancho Gil, 2001, p. 144). No doubt tapping into the vast experience of its members, it also carried out an insightful analysis about where the world would and should be heading over the decades to come and what would therefore be the challenges education has to face. The commission identified seven tensions, some of which are still very current, such as between the need of citizens to adopt a global perspective and their urge to stick to their local roots, between the need for competition and the concern for equality of opportunity, or between long-term, often scientifically grounded, and short-term, often politically motivated, considerations that affect policies to be adopted. Overall, according to Tawil and Macedo (2013), "it propos[ed] a *philosophical approach* [emphasis added] to the ultimate purpose of education"; it was a document proposing paradigms for the conceptualisation of an integrated and *humanistic vision of education* [emphasis added]; it "offered a different vision for education from the dominant *utilitarian, economic tone* [emphasis added] prevalent at that time" (pp. 4–5).

The dominance of a utilitarian, economic take on education did not emerge out of nothing. Half a decade before the publication of the Delors report, on November 9, 1989, the Berlin Wall fell. Ostensibly, this marked the end of the Cold War, the antagonism between the "Free World" headed by the United States of America and the world behind what Sir Winston Churchill called the "Iron Curtain,"[15] headed by the Soviet Union. Particularly for the United States, swiftly followed by the Margaret Thatcher ruled Great Britain, the taking down of the Iron Curtain marked the victory of liberal capitalism over socialism and communism. In such a political and economic climate, it is small wonder that the view of education as a humanitarian enterprise, which had dominated in the first postwar decades, had to give in to a view of education as an economic activity, subject to the forces of capital markets. The Delors report may be seen as a final attempt to turn this tide by portraying education as a public good that has a fundamental role to play in personal and social development (Burnett, 2008).

It is safe to conclude then that, by and large, in the last half century, the view of education as a public good that serves humanitarian values has been supplanted by one that sees education as a private good that is subject to market forces.[16] In our view, open universities side with the humanitarian take on education, MOOCs with the utilitarian one. Besides serving different target groups as we already established—learners with an interest in a higher education degree versus learners with an interest in developing themselves professionally—open universities and MOOCs are built on different ideological foundations—humanitarian values versus utilitarian values, in particular, liberal capitalist ones.

CONCLUSION

The prevailing tide of the time, then, is that of liberal capitalist utilitarianism, in which showing solidarity and valuing a sense of community have given way to satisfying one's own needs and taking an individualist perspective. In a recent essay entitled "Inequality and Limits," Bonnie Nardi (2015) convincingly traced a number of undesirable consequences of this type of transition. And as we showed, it is this transition that coincides with the advent of MOOCs as an alternative mode of implementing openness in education, one that is radically different than the kind of openness open universities were built on. Indeed, we suggest that it is the liberal capitalist form of utilitarianism that gave rise to the emergence of MOOCs as we know them. However, true as this may be, the decisive question is whether a utilitarian view of openness and the kinds of MOOCs we discussed as the operationalisation thereof should be a cause for concern?

Our answer is a nuanced but firm 'yes.' We gladly admit that there could well be a place for the kinds of MOOCs we discussed, and only time can tell whether they indeed will be able to carve out a place for themselves in the educational landscape. Much depends on their ability to find sustainable business models. However, we are also convinced that it would be a grave mistake to interpret their current and possible future successes as a sign that a few MOOC providers suffice to serve the worldwide education market, as MOOC proponent Sebastian Thrun initially claimed,[17] that one can do without humanitarian values in education, and that open universities have become relics or worse, should henceforth adopt a utilitarian *modus operandi*.[18]

First, and to reiterate our position, we firmly believe that education without a humanitarian outlook is a gravely impoverished form of education, a form of education that is commensurate with a world without solidarity and compassion, a world that sees monetary values as the most important values. We would not appreciate living in such a world and we believe we are in good company. Delors, in his 1996 report, vehemently tried to retain the humanitarian aspect of education. Similarly, Markus Deimann has been arguing for a while in favour of adopting the German ideal of *Bildung* for open education, *Bildung* being the mould in which the German educational system traditionally casts its humanitarian ideals (Deimann, 2013; Deimann & Farrow, 2013; Deimann & Sloep, 2013). However, being in good company hardly qualifies as a valid argument. What more causes for concern are there?

The first is that in a world in which utilitarian MOOCs are the dominant form of education, students would be confronted with the pedagogy of mastery learning only. MOOCs can't do without that pedagogy, because they need its logic of investing in content development (design time) and not in tutoring (runtime) to be economically viable. The more time is devoted to runtime and the less to design time, the profits that the Internet 'laws' of low reproduction, transaction and distribution costs guarantee, start to crumble. The larger the number of registrants, the more acute this issue becomes. However, mastery learning is a limited and outdated pedagogy. There are good reasons for why alternative pedagogies for the design of MOOC-like online learning are widely discussed (Bayne & Ross, 2014;

Sloep, 2014). One of those is networked learning—social constructivist learning supported by advanced technologies (e.g., Carvalho & Goodyear, 2014; Sloep, 2015)—of which indeed the earliest MOOCs, by Cormier, Downes and Siemens, are an example.

Since MOOCs rely on this pedagogy, there is a danger that a two-tiered educational system will arise—MOOCs and mastery learning for the masses and other course types with more sophisticated and also more labour-intensive pedagogies for those who can afford it. And, indeed, in a widely cited TED talk in 2012, Daphne Koller of Coursera claimed that MOOCs could democratise education.[19] Now recall that for Thrun and Norvig's introductory artificial intelligence class, MOOC students registered from 250 different countries, among them several so-called developing countries. MOOCs would allow students in developing countries, with their ailing educational systems, to have access to content from elite U.S. universities. A similar argument has been made with respect to the educational system in the United States itself, where tuition costs have been on the rise for decades and quality has been going down. A Californian legislator suggested that MOOCs could be the way out of this problem.[20]

Obviously, from a utilitarian point of view, this kind of democratising is entirely justified. However, from a wider moral point of view, it isn't. First, 'helping' troubled educational systems in developing countries by making them superfluous amounts to neocolonialist or cultural imperialism (cf. Sonwalker, Wilson, Ng, & Sloep, 2013).[21] The morally right thing to do would be to help them set up a properly functioning educational system, so that the countries could take responsibility for their own education, students could be taught in their native language and in their own cultural settings. That way, they at least would have a choice. Similarly, in the United States, the higher education system is in such poor shape because public funding has been decreasing for decades, and the increases in tuition fees do not make up for the difference.[22] Small wonder then that the quality has decreased. Here too, the morally right thing to do would be to increase public funding so that every student would have access to a quality education.

Moral philosopher Michael Sandel, in a book entitled *What Money Can't Buy: The Moral Limits of Markets* (2012), extensively discussed these kinds of situations, also outside of education. The essence of what he claimed is that there is a moral limit to what we should put a monetary value on; that is, that there is a limit to commoditisation (as in courses), to privatisation and commercialisation (as in universities). We wholeheartedly agree with this. Although there may well be room for MOOCs, insisting on a utilitarian philosophy to underpin open education or even education *tout court* leads to seriously impoverished forms thereof, forms that make a mockery of the humanitarian values that in our view any education system needs to adopt to remain morally defensible.[23]

Although we firmly stand behind this conclusion of our analysis, we are not impervious to a number of arguments that one may level against it. We will discuss and try to defuse what we believe are the most important ones.

First, one may argue that we have set up a straw man when discussing MOOCs as we did. The original model of the early MOOCs that we discussed earlier has been modified in various ways over the years. Indeed, although the MOOCs we discussed are the most prominent ones of the early days, they were by no means the first. As we indicated in an endnote, they were preceded by the pedagogically more sophisticated connectivist MOOCs of Cormiers, Downes and Siemens, which fit into a tradition of networked learning, their underpinning much more in line with humanitarian than utilitarian principles (McAuley, Stewart, Siemens, & Cormier, 2010; Rodriguez, 2013; Yuan & Powell, 2013). Also, the edX platform that MIT and Harvard set up almost simultaneously with Udacity and Coursera differs significantly from theirs. It is funded out of donations by alumni, strictly not-for-profit, should be seen as a follow up to their October 2001 decision to make their educational resources freely available and is intended to serve the community and to do research on online learning.[24] Finally, recent MOOC initiatives that have emerged in particular in continental Europe—iversity, OpenupEd—like the connectivist MOOCs, combine a more sophisticated pedagogy with an allegiance to humanitarian values. Also, to varying extents, they rely on public funding and therefore are not subject to the demand of making a profit like MOOCs supported by venture capital. Our analysis does not apply or applies only to a limited extent to these types of MOOCs. That said, the Coursera, Udacity and Miriada X MOOCs to which we have directed our objections are the largest ones and are still quite influential.

Second, and restricting ourselves to the utilitarian MOOCs, if you like, one may argue that the picture we paint is too black and white and does not allow for any nuance. For sure, Thrun no longer believes that 50 universities suffice to serve the world, and Koller has publicly recanted her claims about the democratising effect of MOOCs. Also, research is done to mitigate the effects of the mastery learning pedagogical model (to the extent that the utilitarian model is able to absorb such pedagogies). True as this may be, it is the utilitarian value system out of which these MOOCs arose that prompted the remarks by Thrun and Koller and suggested mastery learning as a pedagogy. The fact that the sharpness may have been taken off of their stances and the way the utilitarian MOOCs are deployed has become more palatable, does not detract from the fact that they derive from a value system that is ill-suited for education, a system that in the final analysis denies open education its humanitarian values. This cannot be portrayed but in black-and-white terms as such is the nature of these underlying value systems. Anyone who wants to experiment with MOOCs or investigate their potential for education on their own terms should do so. Still, we would suggest remaining keenly aware of the two contrasting philosophies we described.

Third, how about the other forms of openness? Does our analysis of opposing underlying philosophies and value systems apply to them as well? Lack of space prevents us from ticking them off one by one and establishing to what extent our analysis applies to them. But actually, we doubt whether such an exercise would make much sense. Thinking about openness is in a state of flux. So rather than declare to what forms our analysis does and does not apply, we would reverse the argument. If what we have said seems to make any sense, we invite others to use our analysis of contrasting underlying philosophies to scrutinise other forms of openness and clarify those forms' position with respect to humanitarian and utilitarian values. OERs, it would seem, are not necessarily aligned with humanitarian or utilitarian values. It is how one wishes to conceptualise them. The exercise of (re)conceptualising forms of openness would seem to be a much more productive one than establishing in some essentialist sense what they are.

The ultimate question is a normative one: Which way do we want that openness in education to go? That question concerns educational resources, open educational practices and what other forms the educational system may spawn. For ultimately, we as stakeholders, in the learning of our children and grandchildren, in the professional development and *Bildung* of ourselves, should get the educational systems that we want, including appropriate forms of openness therein. Every individual then should decide for herself or himself to what extent this requires education as a public good and to what extent education as a private good, that is, as a commodity subject to market forces. It should not come as a surprise that we side with the humanitarian elaboration of openness. Indeed, we feel that governments as guardians of the public space should actively get involved in promoting this kind of openness, indeed, much as Delors in 1996 advocated for education as a whole.

NOTES

1. The University of South Africa was already established in 1873. It did and does embrace open distance learning, but it never advertised itself as an open university.
2. This type of information can be verified at the universities' web sites, the pages that Wikipedia features on them and in part also at the site of the *European Association of Distance Teaching Universities* (EADTU; http://www.eadtu.eu/members/current-members) and at the site of the *International Council for Open and Distance Education* (ICDE; http://www.icde.org/institutions).
3. At The Open University of the Netherlands (OUNL), the total fee each individual student pays to obtain a degree is roughly equivalent to the tuition students in traditional universities pay. But there are lots of assumptions here. Students at OUNL pay per course, whereas students

at traditional universities pay per year or semester. A slow student at a traditional university therefore quickly ends up paying more than an OUNL student. On the other hand, students at traditional universities are eligible for student loans, which OUNL students are not. Data on The Open University of the Netherlands are provided by the authors themselves, one of whom is and the other was for several years employed by the university.
4. 'Traditional universities' is a term that is often used to denote universities that are not 'open.' Traditional universities, then, mostly cater to adolescents and have brick and mortar buildings where students and staff meet.
5. The yearly eMOOCs conference, started in 2013, is an example of a conference that is fully devoted to MOOCs. Liyanagunawardena, Adams, and Williams (2013) carried out a review of MOOC-related articles published between 2008 and 2012. Following are a few special issues: *International Review of Research in Open and Distance Learning*, *12*(3), 2011; *Journal of Online Learning with Technology*, *9*(2), 2013; *Journal of Distance Education*, *35*(2), 2014; *Comunicar*, *22*(44), 2015. Following are several projects funded by the European Union and devoted to MOOCs: *European Multiple MOOC Aggregator, MOOCKnowledge, Higher Education Online: MOOCs the European Way*.
6. Much of MOOC history is 'common knowledge', shared in blogs (e.g., http://www.scoop.it/t/networked-learning-learning-networks/ or http://www.scoop.it/t/openingupuducation), articles in *The New York Times* (http://www.nytimes.com/2011/08/16/science/16stanford.html), *Inside Higher Ed*, *The Chronicle of Higher Education*, *Wired* (http://www.wired.com/2012/03/ff_aiclass/) and so on. The MOOC lemma in the English version of Wikipedia does a good job of consolidating much of this information (https://en.wikipedia.org/wiki/Massive_open_online_course).
7. Strictly speaking, there is another type of MOOC that predated them, set up by Cormier, Downes, and Siemens. We come back to these later. See also Yuan and Powell (2013).
8. It was generally thought, and with good reason, that part of the success of the early MOOCs was the idea of being able to develop a course with an 'elite' university at no cost.
9. According to Sara Custer, on August 27, 2014, in *The Pie News*, which provides news and business analysis for professionals in international education (http://thepienews.com/news/spanish-portuguese-mooc-platform-rolled-latin-america/).
10. See http://www.economist.com/news/business/21582001-army-new-online-courses-scaring-w its-out-traditional-universities-can-they.
11. See, for example, http://techcrunch.com/2013/01/08/coursera-takes-a-big-step-toward-mon etization-now-lets-students-earn-verified-certificates-for-a-fee/ and https://about.futurelearn .com/about/faq/
12. See an article on the topic of business models for MOOCs in *Inside Higher Ed:* https://www .insidehighered.com/news/2012/06/11/experts-speculate-possible-business-models-mooc-prov iders.
13. The declaration was adopted by a vote of 48 in favour, none against, and eight abstentions (Soviet Union, Ukraine, Byelorussia, Yugoslavia, Poland, Union of South Africa, Czechoslovakia, Saudi Arabia; see http://www.un.org/en/documents/udhr/).
14. See http://www.nobelprize.org/nobel_prizes/peace/laureates/2012/.
15. Ignace Feuerlicht apparently coined this term in October 1955: A New Look at the Iron Curtain, *American Speech*, *30*(3), 186–189.
16. Fear that this type of transition was lying in wait was already voiced by one of us in a late 2012 blogpost: http://pbsloep.blogspot.nl/2012/11/moocs-what-about-them.html.

17. According to the *Wired* article already mentioned, "Fifty years from now, according to Thrun, there will be only 10 institutions in the whole world that deliver higher education" (see http://www.wired.com/2012/03/ff_aiclass/).
18. The first signs of such a move are already showing themselves. Funding for The Open University of the Netherlands, for example, is dependent on 'output' in terms of the number of students who graduate. Funding is in part dependent on 'efficiency,' the time it takes those students to graduate. Underlying considerations are 'returns on (public) investment' and 'time to market.' These are economic considerations in which there is no room for, say, the contribution that individual courses have on citizenship education, let alone personal development.
19. For Koller's Ted talk, see http://www.ted.com/talks/daphne_koller_what_we_re_learning_from_online_education.
20. See an article by Paul Fain and Ry Rivard in *Inside Higher Ed:* https://www.insidehighered.com/news/2013/03/13/california-bill-encourage-mooc-credit-public-colleges For a nuanced view, see the following Inside Higher Ed article by Ryan Craig: https://www.insidehighered.com/views/2012/08/31/massive-open-courses-arent-answer-reducing-higher-ed-inequality-essay.
21. See also http://pbsloep.blogspot.nl/2013/11/moocs-democratising-education-i-am-not.html
22. See, for example, http://www.bloomberg.com/news/articles/2014-11-13/college-tuition-in-the-u-s-again-rises-faster-than-inflation. Wikipedia also has an insightful lemma: https://en.wikipedia.org/wiki/College_tuition_in_the_United_States.
23. For a slightly more extensive analysis of the relevance of Sandel's ideas for MOOCs, see http://pbsloep.blogspot.nl/2013/01/moocs-what-about-them-continued.html
24. Personal communication by Katie Vale (see http://pbsloep.blogspot.nl/2012/10/how-to-improve-teaching-with.html).

REFERENCES

Anderson, C. (2009). *The longer long tail; how endless choice is creating unlimited demand* (2nd ed.). London, UK: Random House Business Books.

Atkins, D. E., Brown, J. S., & Hammond, A. L. (2007). *A review of the open educational resources (OER) movement: Achievements, challenges, and new opportunities* [Special issue]. Review: Literature and Arts of the Americas, 79. doi:10.1128/MCB.05690-11.

Bayne, S., & Ross, J. (2014). *The pedagogy of the massive open online course: The UK view.* York, UK: The Higher Education Academy.

Burnett, N. (2008). The Delors report: A guide towards education for all. *European Journal of Education, 43*(2), 181–187. doi:10.1111/j.1465-3435.2008.00347.x.

Carvalho, L., & Goodyear, P. M. (2014). *The architecture of productive learning networks.* New York, NY: RoutledgeFalmer.

Deimann, M. (2013). Open education and Bildung as kindred spirits. *E-Learning and Digital Media, 10*(2), 190–199.

Deimann, M., & Farrow, R. (2013). Rethinking OERs and their use: Open education as Bildung. *The International Review of Research in Open and Distance Learning, 14*(3), 344–360. Retrieved from http://irrodl.us1.list-manage.com/track/click?u=d5e8b9866b8a89a545c675602&id=b0f14846f7&e=3d67b398c4

Deimann, M., & Sloep, P. B. (2013). How does open education work? In A. Meiszner & L. Squires (Eds.), *Advances in digital education and lifelong learning: Volume 1: Openness and education* (pp. 1–24). Bingley, UK: Emerald Group.

Dellarocas, C., & Van Alstyne, M. (2013). Money models for MOOCs: Considering new business models for massive open online courses. *Communications of the ACM, 56*(8), 25–28. doi:10.1145/2492007.

Delors, J. (1996). Learning: The treasure within: Report to the UNESCO of the International Commission on Education for the Twenty-first Century. *United Nations Scientific and Cultural Organisation, UNESCO.* Retrieved from http://unesdoc.unesco.org/images/0010/001095/109590eo.pdf

Falconer, I., McGill, L., Littlejohn, A., & Boursinou, E. (2013). Overview and analysis of practices with open educational resources in adult education in Europe. *European Commission Joint Research Centre Institute for Prospective Technological Studies, 1–82.* doi:10.2791/34193.

Faure, E., Herrera, F., Kaddoura, A.-R., Lopes, H., Petrovsky, A. V., Rahnema, M., & Ward, F. C. (1972). *Learning to be. The world of education today and tomorrow.* Paris, France: UNESCO. Retrieved from http://unesdoc.unesco.org/images/0000/000018/001801e.pdf

Gaebel, M. (2014). *MOOCs: Massive open online courses: An update.* Brussels, Belgium: European University Association. doi:10.1093/intimm/dxu021.

Garreta-Domingo, M., Hernández-Leo, D., Mor, Y., & Sloep, P. B. (2015, September 15–18). Teachers' perceptions about the HANDSON MOOC: A Learning Design Studio case. In G. Conole, C. Rensing, J. Konert, & D. Hutchison (Eds.), *Design for teaching and learning in a networked world. Proceedings of the 10th European Conference on Technology Enhanced Learning, EC-TEL 2015 Toledo, Spain* (pp. 420–427). Berlin, Germany: Springer.

Grainger, B. (2013). *Massive open online course (MOOC) report.* London, UK: University of London.

Hill, B. V. (1975). What's open about open education? In D. Nyberg (Ed.), *The philosophy of open education* (pp. 3–13). New York Routledge & Kegan Paul.

Judt, T. (2005). *Postwar: A history of Europe since 1945.* New York, NY: The Penguin Press. doi:10.1086/596674.

Liyanagunawardena, T. R., Adams, A. A., & Williams, S. A. (2013). MOOCs: A systematic study of the published literature 2008–2012. *The International Review of Research in Open and Distance Learning, 14*(3), 202–227. doi:10.3329/bjms.v12i4.16658.

Mak, G. (2004). *In Europa: Reizen door de twintigste eeuw* [In Europe: Travelling through the twentieth century]. Amsterdam, The Netherlands: Atlas.

McAuley, A., Stewart, B., Siemens, G., & Cormier, D. (2010). *The MOOC model for digital practice.* Retrieved from http://www.elearnspace.org/Articles/MOOC_Final.pdf

Meadows, D. H., Meadows, D. L., Randers, J., & Behrens, W. W. (1972). *The limits to growth.* New York, NY: Universe Books.

Mulder, F., & Jansen, D. (2015). MOOCs for opening up education and the OpenupEd initiative. In C. J. Bonk, M. M. Lee, T. C. Reeves, & T. H. Reynolds (Eds.), *The MOOCs and open education around the world* (pp. xx–yy). New York, NY: Taylor & Francis. Retrieved from http://www.eadtu.eu/documents/Publications/OEenM/OpenupEd_-_MOOCs_for_opening_up_educat ion.pdf

Mulder, F., & Janssen, B. (2013). Opening up education. In R. Jacobi, H. Jelgerhuis, & N. Van der Woert (Eds.), *Trend report: Open educational resources 2013* (pp. 36–42). Utrecht, The Netherlands: SURF.

Nardi, B. A. (2015). Inequality and limits. *First Monday, 20*(8).

Nyberg, D. (1975). *The philosophy of open education*. London, UK: Routledge & Kegan Paul. doi:10.2307/3119916.
Peter, S., & Deimann, M. (2013). On the role of openness in education: A historical reconstruction. *Open Praxis*, 5(1), 7–14. doi:10.5944/openpraxis.5.1.
Rodriguez, O. (2013). The concept of openness behind c and x-MOOCs (massive open online courses). *Open Praxis*, 5(1), 67–73. doi:10.5944/openpraxis.5.1.42.
Sancho Gil, J. M. (2001). Hacia una visión compleja de la Sociedad de la Información y sus implicaciones para la educación. In F. Blazquez Entonado (Ed.), *Sociedad de la informacion y educacion* (pp. 140–158). Mérida, Spain: Junta de Extremadura, Consejeria de Educacion, Ciencia y Tecnologie. Retrieved from http://www.quadernsdigitals.net/datos_web/biblioteca/l_1400/enLinea/9.pdf
Sandel, M. J. (2012). *What money can't buy: The moral limits of markets*. New York, NY: Farrar, Straus and Giroux.
Schuwer, R., van Genuchten, M., & Hatton, L. (2015). On the impact of being open. *IEEE Software*, 32(5), 81–83. Retrieved from http://www.computer.org/csdl/mags/so/2015/05/mso2015050081.html
Sloep, P. B. (2013). Networked professional learning. In A. Littlejohn & A. Margaryan (Eds.), *Technology-enhanced professional learning: Processes, practices and tools* (pp. 97–108). London, UK: Routledge. Retrieved from http://hdl.handle.net/1820/5215
Sloep, P. B. (2014). Didactic methods for open and online education. In H. Jelgerhuis & R. Schuwer (Eds.), *Open and online education; special edition on didactics* (pp. 15–18). Utrecht, The Netherlands: SURF. Retrieved from http://www.surf.nl/binaries/content/assets/surf/en/knowledgebase/2014/special-edition-on-didactics-of-open-and-online-education.pdf
Sloep, P. B. (2015). Design for networked learning. In B. Gros, Kinshuk, & M. Maina (Eds.), *The future of ubiquitous learning: Learning designs for emerging pedagogies* (pp. 41–58). Berlin, Germany: Springer. doi:10.1007/978-3-662-47724-3_3.
Sloep, P. B., Berlanga, A. J., Greller, W., Stoyanov, S., Van der Klink, M. R., Retalis, S., & Hensgens, J. (2012). Educational innovation with learning networks: Tools and developments. *Journal of Universal Computer Science*, 18(1), 44–61. doi:10.3217/jucs-017-01-0044.
Sonwalkar, N., Wilson, J., Ng, A., & Sloep, P. B. (2013). Roundtable discussion, state-of-the-field discussion. *MOOCs Forum*, 1, 6–9. doi:10.1089/mooc.2013.0006.
Tawil, S., & Macedo, B. (2013). Revisiting learning: The treasure within: Assessing the influence of the 1996 Delors report. *UNESCO Education Research and Foresight, Occasional Papers*, 4, 1–9.
Wubbels, T. (2014). *Verbeter het onderwijs: Begin niet alleen bij de docent* [Improve education: Don't start with the teacher only]. Utrecht, the Netherlands: Utrecht University. Retrieved from http://dspace.library.uu.nl/handle/1874/299638/
Yuan, L., & Powell, S. (2013). *MOOCs and open education: Implications for higher education*. Bolton, UK. Retrieved from http://publications.cetis.ac.uk/2013/667

CHAPTER SEVEN

Another World Is Possible: The Relationship Between Open Higher Education AND Mass Intellectuality

RICHARD HALL

Since the economic crisis of 2007 the politics of austerity has subsumed academic and student labour across the higher education (HE) sector in the global North (Hall, 2015a; McGettigan, 2013; Winn, 2015). One outcome is that this labour is conditioned by the interrelationships between first, lives that are conditioned by productivity, and second, the use of high technology to proletarianise educational work (Basu & Vasudevan, 2011; Bellamy Foster & Yates, 2014). Across the HE sector, this process of conditioning is realised through, for instance, internationalisation strategies like open education and massive open on-line courses (MOOCs), a recalibration of curricula around student entrepreneurialism, the use of performance management techniques and learning analytics and a rapid increase in institutional and student debt (Crawford, 2014). In terms of the political economy of HE, these innovations are used to overcome the barriers to the production, circulation and accumulation of surplus value in that sector. As a result, HE and the university become a means for the production of value, as well as enabling the calibration of national and transnational relations of production (Byrne, 2014; Hancock, 2014).

In this analysis, the idea of HE is incorporated inside a cultural turn toward entrepreneurialism and competition, which are themselves immanent to processes of financialisation and marketisation (Davies, 2014; McGettigan, 2013). The interplay between financialisation and marketisation reproduces the relationships, outputs and impact of academic labour as commodities that are stripped of their humane content through the pressures of proletarianisation (Bain & Company, 2012; Regalado & Leber, 2013; Rizvi, Donnelly, & Barber, 2013). These pressures operate globally and are influenced both by national educational policy like indentured study and using HE as an export strategy, and internationally through the role of trade partnerships and innovations like MOOCs (Carnegie Associates, 2014; Haggard, 2013). Inside the university in the global North, this has led to the attrition of the labour rights of precariously employed academics and graduate students, and professional services' staff (CASA, 2015; 3cosas, 2015). Thus, in the process of contending and competing globally, academic labour is increasingly subsumed under the law of value, which demands the generation of academic services that can be commodified as technological, entrepreneurial and impactful, and exchanged globally (Marx, 1992).

This reproduction of academic labour under the law of value, in order that it becomes productive, points to a future where both the student and the academic become self-exploiting entrepreneurs (Richmond, 2014). In this frame, the relations of production pivot around the promise of autonomy and ever-increasing standards of living, whilst in reality they underscore longer working hours and the attrition of wages and labour rights in the face of widening inequality (Bellamy Foster & Yates, 2014; Jimeno, Smets, & Yiangou, 2014). This echoes Marx and Engels' (2002) argument that the expansion of value, driven by space-time compression across an international market, would proletarianise increasing amounts of work. In a competitive, transnational, educational market, historic conceptions of public education are threatened by the equalising pressures of transnational competition and productivity, which includes new forms of competition from private providers with degree-awarding powers, partnerships of accrediting organisations operating through MOOCs, or hedge funds providing venture capital for technologically driven innovations (Ball, 2012; Hall, 2015b).

It is against this structuring reality of the subsumption of academic labour inside the law of value that a reappraisal of open education might emerge. The point of such a reappraisal is to elaborate the role and character of open education and its relationship to academic labour, to describe how its existing forms might be transcended. This chapter develops an analysis of how open education forms one strand of a global response to the secular crisis of capitalism (Hall, 2015a). It then describes the relationship between open education and the idea of public HE. In describing this relationship and the concomitant potential for transcending value relations, the chapter uses the concept of mass intellectuality as a pivot for developing alternatives (Bologna, 2014; Cleaver, 2000; Marx, 2004; Tomba & Bellofiore, 2014; Virno, 2001). Finally, these alternatives are situated against the possibilities that emerge from open cooperativism as a political, pedagogic project for the liberation of time (Conaty & Bollier, 2015; Hall, 2014; Winn, 2015).

OPEN EDUCATION AND THE PROLETARIANISATION OF HIGHER EDUCATION

In his recent work on neoliberalism, Davies (2014) provided a frame for analysing capitalist work inside HE, in light of self-exploiting entrepreneurial activity that is increasingly fractured (Richmond, 2014). Such activity is

- Enacted through new combinations of technologies and practices to inject novelty into the circuits of capitalism.
- Operating through counteracting norms that can never be stabilised.
- Rooted in a new productive environment that accommodates power: first in expanding the time-scale for returns; second in expanding the arena for competition.
- Grounded in ideas of vision and desire.

In this model, educational innovation is the recalibration of academic labour as entrepreneurial to widen the orbit of productive labour. In this way, it reproduces capitalist relations of production whilst reimagining how the forces of production might be revolutionised. In part, this is achieved through the entrepreneurial endeavour of the individual. However, across HE, it is also achieved through the entrepreneurial recalibration of the university as a site for the reproduction of collective labour. Critically, this means that universities as businesses are restructured for the production of surplus value, through organisational development, knowledge transfer, impact, technological innovation, digital literacy strategies and so on. As the information technology consultancy Gartner noted (2013), this tends toward the increasing proletarianisation of work:

> Digitization is reducing labor content of services and products in an unprecedented way, thus fundamentally changing the way remuneration is allocated across labor and capital…. Mature economies will suffer most as they don't have the population growth to increase autonomous demand nor powerful enough labor unions or political parties to (re-)allocate gains in what continues to be a global economy.

This has a direct connection to the idea advanced by Marx and Engels (2002), that the logic of the law of value compels businesses to compete technologically to reduce the costs of labour and to expand the absolute space-time of value production (Harvey, 2010). On a global terrain, this expansion of the forces of production has implications for the relations of production and for class composition that impacts the space-time of HE.

> The bourgeoisie cannot exist without constantly revolutionising the instruments of production, and thereby the relations of production, and with them the whole relations of

society.... Constant revolutionising of production, uninterrupted disturbance of all social conditions, everlasting uncertainty and agitation distinguish the bourgeois epoch from all earlier ones. All fixed, fast-frozen relations, with their train of ancient and venerable prejudices and opinions, are swept away, all new-formed ones become antiquated before they can ossify. All that is solid melts into air, all that is holy is profaned, and man is at last compelled to face with sober senses his real conditions of life, and his relations with his kind. (Marx & Engels 2002, p. 223)

Such rapid entrepreneurial activity across globalised HE can be read as a response by capital to a secular crisis of capitalism, which is characterised by liquidity traps, high public and private debt, weak levels of investment and aggregate demand and ongoing weak or no growth. Keynesian analyses of this crisis have argued that slow population growth in the global North, lower levels of educational attainment, rising levels of inequality and massive levels of public and private debt have acted as brakes on the global economy. One implication has been the rollback of labour rights alongside privatisation that enforces market efficiencies to regear economic activity through total factor productivity or human capital theory (Hall, 2015a).

For HE, this has catalysed a process of marketisation through which entrepreneurs can be persuaded to invest. In part, investment opportunities are rooted in open access, *both* to the data *and* to the services produced in HE (Bain & Company, 2012; Department of Business Innovation and Skills [DBIS], 2014; Hancock, 2014; Willetts, 2014), so that they can be commodified and rents exacted from them. Underscored by open access, education-as-a-service becomes a positional good, rooted in the exchange value of specific commodities (McGettigan, 2013) and in the motivation of individuals to invest in their own education, skills and productivity (Davies, 2014). One other critical facet of this response is the opening up of state-sponsored infrastructures for investment through a transnational educational policy framework (Gates Foundation, 2014; Robinson, 2004; World Bank, 2011). The marketisation of HE then enables narratives of openness in educational contexts, of open forms of educational provision or of open access to public HE, to be normalised inside the law of value.

The imperative for open access to education-as-a-service emerges as a response to the secular crisis and underpins a belief that ongoing stagnation is amplified by poorly functioning competition and global markets (Bellamy Foster & Yates, 2014; Jimeno et al., 2014). For Carchedi and Roberts (2013), this is pivotal because the heart of the crisis is the collapse of production for profit by the private owners of the means of production. Here, the crisis emerges immanent to collapse in global rates of profit, and recovery demands sufficient creative destruction of unproductive capital (Schumpeter, 1975). This is one reason why corporations have no motivation to invest in new capital or professional development (Broadbent, 2012). In this model, the slide in productivity and the ongoing weakness of growth in the global North demonstrate the persistent inability of surplus capital to recombine with surplus labour, to valorise itself.

A critical frame for the analysis of open forms of educational practice is a countermeasure to this secular crisis of capitalism and its subsumption of HE inside the law of value. This focus on productivity and efficiency, through marketisation and financialisation, restructures the form and content of academic work as a commodity that can be exchanged, rather than a socially useful product. Policy encourages the opening up of education-as-a-service for commercialisation and to amplify potential *spillovers* from HE into other sectors (DBIS, 2014; Hancock, 2014). In research, knowledge transfer, impact metrics, bibliometrics and open data sets enable commercialisation. In teaching and learning, curriculum content or the licensing of open educational resources (OER) alongside learning analytics enables new financial products to be traded (McGettigan, 2013) and commodity dumping from the global North into the global South (Hall, 2015b). These products have *both* a use value, in that they enable someone to do something useful or extend knowledge for its own sake, *and* an exchange value, in that they can be exchanged for other commodities, including money (Willetts, 2014). It is the transnational exchange value of academic commodities, including academic labour power, which enables universities to compete and which drives engagement with open education-as-a-service. Open education, in the governing principles that shape the content and forms that it takes, emerges from the potential exchange value of academic labour and the relationship among academic commodities (Wendling, 2009).

A move toward open practices inside HE in the global North is a tactical countermeasure designed to overcome the limits to accumulation imposed through the secular crisis (Cleaver, 1993) and to encourage self-exploiting entrepreneurial activity. These countermeasures include the following: the opening up of academic data, including learning analytics for commercialisation (Bain & Company, 2012; Willetts, 2013); the licensing and distribution of OER under commercial, attribution licences (Haggard, 2013; Holmwood, 2013); and the creation of open learning environments like MOOCs, as an export strategy (Hall, 2015b; World Bank, 2011). The cultural turn inside HE toward the idea of open commodities, to openness as an organising principle, or to open education-as-a-service, might usefully be situated against the following questions.

1. How is it possible to reimagine open education to overcome proletarianisation through technologised, self-exploiting entrepreneurial activity?
2. How might open education broaden the horizon of political possibility inside and beyond HE, as a pedagogic project?

OPEN EDUCATION AND MASS INTELLECTUALITY

The potential for reimagining the idea of open education might usefully be described in relation to 'mass intellectuality' as a mechanism for framing a socially useful open education. Such an approach recognises how open education is alienated as it emerges immanent to the proletarianisation of the university. Mass intellectuality is important because it enables an analysis of the organising principles, governance and production of open education as a form of living, socially useful knowledge. Mass intellectuality has its origins within the autonomist Marxist tradition, building on Marx's conceptualisation of the 'general intellect' (Dyer-Witheford, 1999; Marx, 1993; Virno, 2001). Marx (1993) argued that the development of the forces of production mean

> the accumulation of knowledge and of skill, of the general productive forces of the social brain, is thus absorbed into capital, as opposed to labour, and hence appears as an attribute of capital, and more specifically of fixed capital [machinery]. (p. 694)

Through entrepreneurial activity, innovation and the compulsion of competition, the technical and skilled work of the socialised worker, operating in factories, corporations, schools and so on, is incorporated inside machinery. As a result, the 'general intellect' of society as its productive capacity and capability is absorbed into capitalised technologies and techniques to reduce labour costs and to increase productivity. One outcome is proletarianisation, as the form and content of science and technology inside capitalist work and the ways in which they are organised, reduces labouring to a process of regulating the production process (Marx, 1993, p. 705).

Inside the crisis of funding, regulation and governance of public HE, there is a need to understand the mechanisms through which the general intellect is co-opted to enable value production (Virno, 2004) and how open education contributes to that co-option. Addressing the secular crisis and the concomitant subsumption of HE in this way enables a focus on the production of alternative educational practices, which are themselves reimaginings of the idea of what HE might be for. These alternatives are rooted in the potential for reclaiming and liberating the knowledge, skills, practices and techniques that form the general intellect to produce and circulate new forms of socially useful knowledge or ways of knowing the world. From this reclaiming or liberation of the general intellect emerges 'mass intellectuality,' as a direct, social force of production (Bologna, 2014; Thorburn, 2012; Tomba & Bellofiore, 2014; The University of Utopia, 2015; Virno, 2004). This hinges on the production of a "direct form of communal manifestations of life carried out in association with others—[that] are therefore an expression and confirmation of that social life" (Marx & Engels, 2011, p. 74).

Aligning open education with mass intellectuality demands a more critical discussion of the possibilities for open pedagogic production as an activity that is for society rather than for profit. Here, models of the distributed, collective production of knowledge, and the potential for distributed, cooperative education, rooted in the growing social subjectivity of cooperative labour, are central. Yet open education is also conditioned by the absorption and objectification of that collective work inside the structuring realities of capitalist social relations, which commodifies open education-as-a-service. In analysing the relationships between open education and mass intellectuality, the idea of overcoming or transcending those relations of production is critical. This is the liberation of the general intellect from its incorporation inside dead labour, so that it is available for living labour to reclaim our shared humanity.

> Central to Marx's conception of the overcoming of capitalism is his notion of people's reappropriation of the socially general knowledge and capacities that had been constituted historically as capital. We have seen that, according to Marx, such knowledge and capacities, as capital, dominate people; such re-appropriation, then, entails overcoming the mode of domination characteristic of capitalist society, which ultimately is grounded in labor's historically specific role as a socially mediating activity. Thus, at the core of his vision of a postcapitalist society is the historically generated possibility that people might begin to control what they create rather than being controlled by it. (Postone, 1996, p. 373)

The struggle for open education as a form of mass intellectuality is an attempt to build solidarity and sharing related to the social and cooperative use of the knowledge, skills and practices that are created as labour. The University of Utopia (2015) argued as follows:

> Mass intellectuality is based on our common ability to do, based on our needs and capacities and what needs to be done. What needs to be done raises doing from the level of the individual to the level of society.

Liberating science and technology from *inside and against* capital's competitive dynamics is central to moving *beyond* exploitation. Inside critical and cooperative (rather than co-opted) educational contexts, the processes of learning and teaching offer the chance to critique the purposes for which the general intellect is commodified rather than made public. They offer the opportunity to reclaim and liberate the general intellect for cooperative use.

At issue is whether open education as an emancipatory project can reappropriate the means of knowledge production in the labour process and describe pedagogic models that nurture the potential for more democratic or cooperative relations of production to emerge (Cleaver, 2000). Here, mass intellectuality as a form of open practice might deterritorialise existing open practices and structures in HE and reclaim a level of productive, scientific and social knowledge as an immanent, transgressive potentiality across capitalist societies (hooks, 1994). As a result, meaningful critiques of open education might then question whether HE can be liberated from the market or from the production of education-as-a-service that can be valorised. The point is to generate the kinds of open practices which are self-challenging and capable of enabling socially useful knowledge production. Mass intellectuality points toward a cooperative respect for social knowledge and the potential for problem solving rooted in coproduction, cocritique and evidential exploration. Mass intellectuality becomes a way of describing *both* the objective conditions through which the products and processes of HE are alienated from their social utility (Mészáros, 2005) *and* the ways in which new relations of production though education might transcend such alienation.

OPEN EDUCATION AND OPEN COOPERATIVISM

One mechanism by which open education might be critiqued as a form of mass intellectuality is through the idea of open cooperativism. This form of open practice is an applied, alternative relation of production that spans the market, the State, the Commons, peer and gift economies and voluntary organisations (Conaty & Bollier, 2015; Winn, 2015). Conaty and Bollier (2015) stated the following:

> "Cooperative accumulation" could occupy a space between commons that have limited or no engagement with markets, and capitalist enterprises that seek to extract private profits and accumulate capital. This intermediary form, open co-operativism, could constitute a new sector in which commoners might pool resources, allocate them fairly and sustainably, and earn livelihoods as members of cooperatives—more or less outside of conventional capitalist markets. What we envisage here is the creation and nurturing of new types of non-capitalist or post-capitalist markets that re-embeds them in social communities and accountability structures. (p. 4)

Open cooperativism emerges from cooperative forms of accumulation that work against either artificially imposed, immaterial scarcities or the pseudoabundance of debt, whilst at the same time working for negotiated, communal ends. A refocusing of production around transitional spaces is seen to be critical in moving beyond the hegemony of the labour theory of value. Inside spaces that are rooted in cooperative organising principles, it is the spread of knowledge at levels that are socially useful that might enable open pedagogies to become a form of mass intellectuality that refuses and pushes back against private accumulation (The Social Science Centre, 2015; Virno, 2001; Winn, 2015).

Such a critical, open, cooperative pedagogy offers the opportunity to move beyond the subordination of the individual's capacity to produce to the division of labour. This means recombining cognitive and kinaesthetic practices so that individuals and the communities in which they live, work and educate might develop beyond their labour power as a commodity with an exchange value. The potential for mass intellectuality emerges

> after the productive forces have also increased with the all-around development of the individual, and all the springs of co-operative wealth flow more abundantly—only then can the narrow horizon of bourgeois right be crossed in its entirety and society inscribe on its banners: From each according to his ability, to each according to his needs! (Marx, 1875)

The ability to critique open education in light of open cooperativism enables the deliberate politicisation of open education's subsumption inside processes of marketisation and financialisation. It is here that the relations of production that are revealed through open education might be used to describe new class compositions, which themselves connect academic labour into society in general. This stands asymmetrically against open education as a means of consumption of education-as-a-service. For instance, from an open and cooperative position it is possible to describe the licensing of OER and the terms of use of open data, in relation to capitalist property rights. An open cooperative model for education points toward ways of reorganising the production, distribution and consumption of HE at the intersection of market, the State, the Commons, peer and gift economies and voluntary organisations. Marx (1875) noted the following:

> Within the co-operative society based on common ownership of the means of production, the producers do not exchange their products; just as little does the labor employed on the products appear here as the *value* of these products, as a material quality possessed by them, since now, in contrast to capitalist society, individual labor no longer exists in an indirect fashion but directly as a component part of total labor.

This interrelationship between the social and individual labourer, and between social and individual time, is immanent to forms of cooperative governance. In defining alternative, political and pedagogical spaces inside which HE might be repurposed for mass intellectuality, Winn (2015) argued that fusing the democratic regulation of transnational worker cooperatives with the circuits of production and distribution of the peer-to-peer economy points toward a counterhegemonic, open cooperative set of possibilities. In terms of open education, cooperative governance has the potential to connect to the open, democratic, autonomous, social focus of cooperatives that have education at their heart. Cooperative governance contributes to the following: the reclamation of public, open environments that enable the globalised, socialised dissemination of knowledge (Kleiner, 2014); the connection of a global set of educational commons rooted in critical pedagogy (Cumbers, 2012; Dyer-Witheford, 1999; FLOK Society, 2014); and the development of relations of production that ground, critique and disseminate the community building of alternative educational settings like cooperative or autonomous centres (Amsler & Neary, 2012).

It is important to note that in the intersection among open education, mass intellectuality and open cooperativism, digital technologies emerge as a way of enabling the recomposition of class struggle and for liberating the general intellect. Kleiner (2014) argued that open alternatives emerge from the relations of production that are immanent to globalised forces of production that are both physical and digital:

> We need venture communism, a form of struggle against the continued expansion of property-based capitalism, a model for worker self-organization inspired by the topology of peer-to-peer networks and the historical pastoral commons. (p. 8)

Inside and beyond the classroom, spaces are needed that refuse their co-option for the market and for the accumulation of wealth and power by elites. This includes the following: first, the ways in which public, open education is co-opted by a rentier class that harvests data and sells and resells educational services grounded in those data; second, the ways in which digital technologies are used to maintain alienating structures of domination over teachers and students, through performativity; third, the reduction of collective power and autonomy to issues of personalisation. In these modes, notionally open forms of education risk reducing student and academic autonomy to compensatory consumption and self-exploiting entrepreneurial activity.

What is triggered at this intersection of open education, mass intellectuality and open cooperativism is a reconsideration of the relationship between pedagogy and civil society. The cooperative negotiation of production, distribution and consumption is focused on finding new forms of value that are grounded in human values that are beyond the logic of the market. The question then is what is the role of open education in broadening the horizon of political possibility inside and beyond HE, as a pedagogic project? Is it possible to use open education *against* the use of intellectual property rights as new sources of monopoly power for rentiers, for instance through copyfarleft (Kleiner, 2014)? Is it possible to liberate the general intellect infused as social use values through critical pedagogy to open up new areas of class struggle? Is it possible to develop and protect the social and associational use value of the Commons, as a terrain for producing alternatives (Cumbers, 2012; Dyer-Witheford, 1999)? Is it possible to open up educational possibility through the knowledge commons or free access to higher education, rather than let them be structured through the market?

It is necessary for us to have a more critical understanding of how technological intensity, including the use of digital tools and the development of digital skills through open education, tends to make labour redundant and increases proletarianisation. Just as students and academics embrace the range of technological possibilities of the open commons or of digital production, they also need the tools to face the reality that capital uses technological and organisational innovation to discipline labour and to impose marketisation and financialisation. Capital controls and deploys technology to squeeze value out of labour, be that through new pedagogies for the entrepreneurial self or to leverage strategies for employability or internationalisation. At issue is how collectively we embrace open and cooperative education through democratic pedagogy and organising principles.

CONCLUSION: IS ANOTHER WORLD POSSIBLE?

Marx and Engels (2011) argued the following:

> The externalization of the worker in his product means not only that his labour becomes an object, an external existence, but that it exists outside him, independently of him and alien to him, and begins to confront him as an autonomous power; that the life which he has bestowed on the object confronts him as hostile and alien. (p. 66)

In this view all labour under private property, rather than that which cooperatively shaped an associational and open society, is alienated because one has to exchange one's labour power as a commodity in order to live. This is the logic of commodifying the social and the personal so that it can be monetised. Education is increasingly subsumed inside this process as a response to the secular crisis, as the prevalence of merchants across the compulsory and postcompulsory sectors attests (Bain & Company, 2012; Gates Foundation, 2014; World Bank, 2011). At issue is the extent to which open education reproduces the forces and relations of production of capitalist society. Is it possible instead to reproduce spaces for personal or societal growth and mutuality?

Such a reconsideration of open education in light of cooperative organising principles as a form of socially useful knowledge, or mass intellectuality, would enable the description of open and cooperative education rooted in the following characteristics (Hall, 2014):

- Public HE and its open educational forms can be reconfigured along the lines of the democratic governance and regulation of transnational worker cooperatives.
- Public forms of HE are connected to the circuits of peer-to-peer production and distribution and solidarity economies that support associational democracy.
- Through a focus on organising principles that are negotiated around solidarity, public forms of HE reflect the open, democratic, autonomous and social focus of cooperatives.

- Open and cooperative education defines a framework for the common ownership of products, assets and commodities, across specific communities.
- The governance arrangements that flow from open and cooperative educational spaces represent the reclamation of public environments for the globalised, socialised dissemination of knowledge. In this way, they connect a global set of educational commons rooted in critical, political pedagogy.
- The content of open and cooperative educational spaces forms potential transitional projects that point toward postcapitalism as a social response to the secular crisis.

Increasingly, the idea of 'open' in HE is a contested terrain (Weller, 2014). Open data, open educational resources, openness, open access and so on, are increasingly extracted from education-as-a-service so that they can be commodified and financialised. Here the law of value ensures that academic engagement with these elements of open education is disciplined, with one outcome being the co-option of 'open' as a means of proletarianising academic labour. Resisting this process demands a political economic critique of open education, which is in turn reframed as a form of mass intellectuality rooted in open cooperative principles. The question is whether, in the face of the co-option of the idea of 'open' as a countermeasure to the secular crisis, students and academics are able to work cooperatively across society to develop a counterhegemonic relation to power as a critical, political, pedagogic project.

REFERENCES

Amsler, S., & Neary, M. (2012). Occupy: A new pedagogy of space and time? *The Journal for Critical Education Policy Studies, 10*(2), 106–138.

Bain & Company. (2012, November 14). *A world awash in money*. Retrieved from http://www.bain.com/publications/articles/a-world-awash-in-money.aspx

Ball, S. J. (2012). *Global Education Inc.: New policy networks and the neo-liberal imaginary*. London, UK: Routledge.

Basu, D., & Vasudevan, R. (2011). *Technology, distribution and the rate of profit in the US economy: Understanding the current crisis*. Retrieved from http://people.umass.edu/dbasu/BasuVasudevanCrisis0811.pdf

Bellamy Foster, J., & Yates, M. D. (2014). Piketty and the crisis of neoclassical economics. *Monthly Review*. Retrieved from http://monthlyreview.org/2014/11/01/piketty-and-the-crisis-of-neoclassical-economics/

Bologna, S. (2014). Workerism: An inside view. From the mass-worker to self-employed labour. In M. v. d. Linden & K. H. Roth (Eds.), *Beyond Marx: Theorising the global labour relations of the twenty-first century* (pp. 121–144). Leiden, the Netherlands: Brill.

Broadbent, B. (2012). *Costly capital and the risk of rare disasters.* London, UK: The Bank of England. Retrieved from http://www.bankofengland.co.uk/publications/Documents/speeches/2012/speech581.pdf

Byrne, L. (2014). *Robbins rebooted: How we earn our way in the second machine age.* London, UK: Social Market Foundation. Retrieved from http://www.smf.co.uk/publications/robbins-rebooted-how-we-earn-our-way-in-the-second-machine-age/

Carchedi, G., & Roberts, M. (2013). A critique of Heinrich's, "crisis theory, the law of the tendency of the profit rate to fall, and Marx's studies in the 1870s." *Monthly Review.* Retrieved from http://monthlyreview.org/commentary/critique-heinrichs-crisis-theory-law-tendency-profit-rate-fall-marxs-studies-1870s

Carnegie Associates. (2014, June). MOOCs: Opportunities for their use in compulsory-age education. *Department for Education Research Report.* Retrieved from https://www.gov.uk/government/uploads/system/uploads/attachment_data/file/315591/DfE_RR355_-_Opportunities_for_MOOCs_in_schools_FINAL.pdf

CASA. (2015). A home online for casual, adjunct, sessional staff and their allies in Australian higher education. Retrieved from http://actualcasuals.wordpress.com/

Cleaver, H. (1993). Theses on secular crisis in capitalism. Retrieved from http://libcom.org/library/theses-secular-crisis-capitalism-cleaver

Cleaver, H. (2000). *Reading capital politically.* Edinburgh: AK Press.

Conaty, P., & Bollier, D. (2015). *Toward an open co-operativism: A new social economy based on open platforms, co-operative models and the commons.* Retrieved from http://bollier.org/sites/default/files/misc-file-upload/files/Open%20Co-operativism%20Report%2C%20January%202015_0.pdf

Crawford, K. (2014, May 30). The anxieties of big data. *The New Inquiry.* Retrieved from http://thenewinquiry.com/essays/the-anxieties-of-big-data/

Cumbers, A. (2012). *Reclaiming public ownership: Making space for economic democracy.* London, UK: Zed Books.

Davies, W. (2014). *The limits of neoliberalism: Authority, sovereignty and the logic of competition.* London, UK: SAGE.

Department of Business Innovation and Skills (DBIS). (2014). *Estimating innovation spillovers: An international sectoral and UK enterprise study.* London, UK: Author. Retrieved from https://www.gov.uk/government/uploads/system/uploads/attachment_data/file/384344/bis-14-1269-estimating-innovation-spillovers-an-international-sectoral-and-uk-enterprise-study.pdf

Dyer-Witheford, N. (1999). *Cyber-Marx: Cycles and circuits of struggle in high-technology capitalism.* Champaign, IL: University of Illinois Press.

FLOK Society. (2014). Open letter to the Commoners. Retrieved from http://en.wiki.floksociety.org/w/Open_Letter_to_the_Commoners

Gartner. (2013, October 8). Gartner reveals top predictions for IT organizations and users for 2014 and beyond. Retrieved from http://gtnr.it/17RLm2v

Gates Foundation. (2014). College-Ready education, strategy overview. Retrieved from http://www.gatesfoundation.org/What-We-Do/US-Program/College-Ready-Education

Haggard, S. (2013). *The maturing of the MOOC* (BIS research paper No. 130). Retrieved from https://www.gov.uk/government/uploads/system/uploads/attachment_data/file/240193/13-1173-maturing-of-the-mooc.pdf

Hall, R. (2014). On the abolition of academic labour: The relationship between intellectual workers and mass intellectuality. *tripleC: Communication, Capitalism & Critique, 12*(2), 822–837. Retrieved from http://triple-c.at/index.php/tripleC/article/view/597

Hall, R. (2015a). The university and the secular crisis. *Open Library of Humanities, 1*(1), e6.

Hall, R. (2015b). For a political economy of massive open online courses. *Learning, Media and Technology, 40*(3), 265–286.

Harvey, D. (2010). *The enigma of capital and the crises of capitalism*. London, UK: Profile Books.

Hancock, M. (2014). *International education strategy*. Retrieved from https://www.gov.uk/government/speeches/international-education-strategy

Holmwood, J. (2013, September/October). Commercial enclosure: Whatever happened to open access? *Radical Philosophy 181*. Retrieved from http://www.radicalphilosophy.com/commentary/commercial-enclosure

hooks, b. (1994). *Teaching to transgress: Education as the practice of freedom*. London, UK: Routledge.

Jimeno, J. F., Smets, F., & Yiangou, J. (2014). Secular stagnation: A view from the Eurozone. In C. Tuelings & R. Baldwin (Eds.), *Secular stagnation: Facts, causes and cures* (pp. 153–164). London, UK: Centre for Economic Policy Research Press.

Kleiner, D. (2014). The telekommunist manifesto. *Network Notebooks 03*. Retrieved from http://www.networkcultures.org/_uploads/%233notebook_telekommunist.pdf

Marx, K. (1875). *Critique of the Gotha Programme*. Retrieved from https://www.marxists.org/archive/marx/works/1875/gotha/ch01.htm

Marx, K. (1992). *Capital, volume 3: A critique of political economy*. London, UK: Penguin.

Marx, K. (1993). *Grundrisse: Outline of the critique of political economy*. London, UK: Penguin.

Marx, K. (2004). *Capital, volume 1: A critique of political economy*. London, UK: Penguin.

Marx, K., & Engels, F. (2002). *The Communist manifesto*. London, UK: Penguin.

Marx, K., & Engels, F. (2011). *Economic and philosophical manuscripts of 1844*. Blacksburg, VA: Wilder.

McGettigan, A. (2013). *The great university gamble: Money, markets and the future of higher education*. London, UK: Pluto Press.

Mészáros, I. (2005). *Marx's theory of alienation*. London, UK: Merlin.

Postone, M. (1996). *Time, labor and social domination: A reinterpretation of Marx's critical theory*. Cambridge, UK: Cambridge University Press.

Regalado, A., & Leber, J. (2013). Intel fuels a rebellion around your data. *MIT Technology Review*. Retrieved from http://www.technologyreview.com/news/514386/intel-fuels-a-rebellion-around-your-data/#ixzz2UfZVIJFE

Richmond, M. (2014, September 6). Unpaid trials & self-exploiting entrepreneurs. *The Occupied Times of London*. Retrieved from http://theoccupiedtimes.org/?p=13436

Rizvi, S., Donnelly, K., & Barber, M. (2013, March). An avalanche is coming: Higher education and the revolution ahead. *Institute for Public Policy Research*. Retrieved from http://www.ippr.org/publications/an-avalanche-is-coming-higher-education-and-the-revolution-ahead

Robinson, W. I. (2004). *A theory of global capitalism: Production, class, and state in a transnational world*. Baltimore, MA: John Hopkins University Press.

Schumpeter, J. A. (1975). *Capitalism, socialism and democracy*. New York, NY: Harper.

The Social Science Centre. (2015). Retrieved from http://socialsciencecentre.org.uk/

Thorburn, E. (2012). Actually existing autonomy and the brave new world of higher education. *Occupied Studies*. Retrieved from http://bit.ly/xzcPRO

3cosas campaign. (2015). Retrieved from http://3cosascampaign.wordpress.com/

Tomba, M., & Bellofiore, R. (2014). The "fragment on machines" and the Grundrisse: The workerist reading in question. In M. v. d. Linden & K. H. Roth (Eds.), *Beyond Marx: Theorising the global labour relations of the twenty-first century* (pp. 345–368). Leiden, the Netherlands: Brill.

The University of Utopia. (2015). *Anti-Curricula: A course of action.* Retrieved from http://www.universityofutopia.org/sharing

Virno, P. (2001). *General intellect.* Retrieved from http://www.generation-online.org/p/fpvirno10.htm

Virno, P. (2004). *A grammar of the multitude.* Los Angeles, CA: Semiotext(e).

Weller, M. (2014). *Battle for open: How openness won and why it doesn't feel like victory.* London, UK: Ubiquity Press. Retrieved from http://dx.doi.org/10.5334/bam

Wendling, A. E. (2009). *Karl Marx on technology and alienation.* London, UK: Palgrave Macmillan.

Willetts, D. (2013). *Robbins revisited: Bigger and better higher education.* London, UK: Social Market Foundation.

Willetts, D. (2014). Contribution of UK universities to national and local economic growth. *Department for Business, Innovation and Skills.* Retrieved from https://www.gov.uk/government/speeches/contribution-of-uk-universities-to-national-and-local-economic-growth

Winn, J. (2015). The co-operative university: Labour, property and pedagogy. *Power and Education, 7*(1), 39–55.

World Bank. (2011). *Education Strategy 2020. Learning for all: Investing in people's knowledge and skills to promote development.* Washington, DC: World Bank. Retrieved from http://siteresources.worldbank.org/EDUCATION/Resources/ESSU/Education_Strategy_4_12_2011.pdf

CHAPTER EIGHT

Open Access, Freedom AND Exclusion

MARTIN OLIVER

Proponents of open education frequently position it as a radical alternative to existing forms of education. Whether discussed in terms of open access to educational materials "enabling universal education" (Caswell, Henson, Jensen, & Wiley, 2008), the possibility that Google searching will end "the monopoly (or at least hegemony)" lecturers and university libraries once embodied (Barber, Donnelly, & Rizvi, 2013, p. 16), or the proposal that MOOCs will replace the need to study for a programme at a 'brick and mortar' campus with a pick and mix selection of "the best online courses from the best professors around the world" (Friedman, 2013), the proposal is that new forms of openness are poised to transform education, sweeping away the constraints of physical sites of learning and solving the problems of educational access for good.

This is hardly a new proposal. As Peter and Deimann (2013) chronicled, sociotechnical developments that affect the 'openness' of education can be traced back to the 12th century. However, the effects of such developments are complex, not simply accumulative, and certainly not a deterministic outcome of technological development. Instead, openness is "not only a technological, but also a social, cultural and economic phenomenon, not bound by institutional or national boundaries. [This shows] the danger of emphasising one aspect of openness while backgrounding others and how unrestricted practices can quickly, and repeatedly, become institutionalized" (Peter & Deimann, 2013, pp. 11–12).

Yet as Peter and Deimann (2013) noted, contemporary discussions of openness seem strangely detached from the past, seeing it instead as a novelty, a new moment in education. Lacking historical context, the development of new technologies may indeed seem to offer a brighter educational future. However, work within the field of educational technology has long been recognized as being caught in cycles of hope, hype and disappointment because it fails to engage adequately with theoretical or historical critique (Mayes, 1995). There is every risk that recent work on open education could repeat this pattern.

At its best, the current hope for openness addresses itself to some of the most pressing political challenges facing education today. Laurillard (2008), for example, focused on the worldwide demand for an estimated additional 125 million higher education places by 2020. Her proposals seek ways "to extend education well beyond the confines of the physical" (p. 321), and ideally, to do so in ways that scale beyond staff to student ratios of 1:30, which even open education programmes have struggled to do. In the last few years, the newspapers would have us believe that massive open online courses (MOOCs) have done exactly that (Lewin, 2012), opening up higher education to over 100,000 students on some early course offerings. Advocates go so far as to claim that the battle for openness has been won and that openness has already become fundamental to higher education (Weller, 2014).

The promise in such proposals is one of universal access—but access to what? What kind of education is envisioned in these accounts? Knox's (2013) discussion of the open educational resources movement noted that universities are described as having functions such as content development, research and credentialing, but teaching methods or teacherly expertise appear to have been dismissed. Weller (2014, pp. 9–12) talked about teachers being relevant when knowledge is scarce but proposed pedagogies of abundance (focused on using abundant online content) and of openness (adding learner networking); "campus classroom based didactic learning pedagogies" (p. 10) are dismissed, wholesale. This account has much to say about connections between learners, and about the generation of more material, but nothing about the value of what is produced or how learners make sense of the abundance they encounter; it addresses provision and access but not the responsibilities that go alongside this. In Ross, Sinclair, Knox, Bayne, and Macleod's (2014) analysis of writing about MOOCs, they argued that peculiarly circumscribed accounts of teachers' roles dominate the discussion. Typically, these are characterised purely in terms of the teacher "having expert knowledge, but lacking the means to widely transmit it" (p. 59). Downes (2011), for example, was quite explicit about this—and about its economic foundations.

> Technology gives us access to new markets. Before the internet, and I remember these days, my power of communication extended to the room that I was in, maybe a bit further

if I shouted, and I did shout from time to time because I wanted to be heard, and that's it. But today, with the various technologies, I have a global reach. I have a global reach not just in terms of distance, I have a global reach in terms of audience. I can reach out beyond my own community, my own group. This is a capacity I never had. (p. 38)

Such writing produces oversimplified views of education—for example, that it is the technologically mediated equivalent of shouting and that Downes's voice can now be heard to the ends of the earth. Consequently, subsequent analysis has resulted in overexaggerated claims for the disruptive potential of MOOCs. This is, arguably, a classic example of Heideggerian enframing: Any aspect of education beyond the need to access information vanishes, leaving only a standing reserve of information resources (which, potentially, includes teachers) waiting to be served up to needy learners.

There are some variations in the scope of such discussions: Writing about cMOOCs, which draw on Connectivist accounts of learning, do draw in slightly different kinds of reserve. In these accounts, cMOOCs are claimed to be "an open and a-hierarchical invitation to participate in and scaffold activities and discussions: a true 'teacher as learner as teacher' model" (McAuley, Stewart, Siemens, & Cormier, 2010, p. 11). In contrast to xMOOCs, fellow participants are foregrounded for their potential in supporting learning; however, the distinctive responsibilities of teachers to plan, coordinate, provide feedback and assess are effaced.

In both these kinds of account, the peculiar enframing of 'education' reduces the account to a matter of information flow. Teaching, as an active, purposeful process, vanishes from the picture, which focuses exclusively and unhelpfully on the learner; it is an example of the 'learnification' of education (Biesta, 2012). Downes (2011, p. 36) was explicit about this, proposing that "the old way is centered around the institution—government, corporation, Microsoft, broadcasting agency, AOL–Time Network—the new way is centered around the individual—the personal website, the blog, the email address." In such accounts, the complexities of educational power are positioned as inherently problematic; they are inherently immoral—rather than historical, perhaps inevitable, maybe even beneficial. They are there to be done away with and certainly not to be explored and understood, as has happened in other areas of research (Ross et al., 2014).

This view of learners as nodes in an information network, sending and receiving information, accords closely with the principles and metaphors that have influenced the design of the Internet and the protocols on which it operates (Friesen, 2010). The development of the Internet has been strongly influenced by funding and projects from the U.S. military, who needed to create distributed networks that would support communication after a nuclear strike. Ironically, given the centrality of the Internet in the open education movement, the view on which this network was developed was one in which humans were treated as a 'processing device,' acting between a machine's display and controls. An important design ideal was to create closed systems, with cybernetic loops improving efficiency through individual feedback—an ideal reminiscent of discussions of personalized learning to this day.

Also ironic, given the stand taken against the power of teachers, is that such discourses are commonly associated with strongly politicized views of the purpose of education. Atkins et al. (2007), for example, discussed "free access to high-quality content to be used by colleges and individuals in the United States and throughout the world to increase human capital" (p. 2). The neoliberal rationale and the geographic bias are plain; as with earlier discussions of flexibility (e.g., Edwards, 1997), learners are compelled to participate or else risk becoming obsolete, unemployable—and thus of no value. Such framing of open access is not universal, of course; for example, Mackie (2008, p. 126) cautioned against exactly this, and Downes (2011) took delight in his anarchic position. However, it serves as a reminder that freedom of access can form part of a wider social project, one in which the freedom *not* to access resources slips away.

A particular problem, according to these accounts, is providing access to infrastructure, and particularly to campuses, libraries and so on (e.g., Lane, 2008; Taylor, 2007). Lane (2008, p. 150), for example, associated the campus with 'closure,' describing using terms such as traditional, boundary, limit, selection, schedule and so on, and stated bluntly that "students must come to the campus to participate in the educational experience"—although he did admit that this portrayal is a "stereotype" (p. 151). Opening access, therefore, is something to be achieved by removing all such restrictions. Technology is the means to achieve this, resulting in a push toward digitization, a focus on access to courseware and above all a denial of the situatedness of studying.

Knox (2013) argued that such positions focus on dismantling hierarchies of control and bypassing the conditions around admittance to knowledge, but they fail to explore what the value of this is to learners. Knox drew on Berlin's differentiation of freedom into positive liberty (where individuals choose the form and quality of freedom they wish to pursue and how to pursue it) and negative liberty (emphasising the removal of barriers to freedom), characterised as freedom *to* and freedom *from*. From this perspective, it becomes clear that these types of accounts focus on forms of negative liberty, shedding 'unfreedoms'; in so doing, they draw attention only to barriers and consequently position institutions as restrictive, exclusionary and self-interested. Moreover, Knox pointed out that an idealistic pursuit of negative liberty would lead to unrestrained action, not to coherent, organised outcomes directly comparable with, or in some enthusiastic accounts even surpassing, those of formal educational systems.

Instead, Knox proposed that adopting a critical theory of the subject would be a more appropriate way to understand open education. This would allow a more nuanced discussion of operations of power, one that acknowledges its inevitable links to claims about knowledge. It would also allow the development of a more coherent account of subjective agency, one able to bring together the purposeful pursuit of individual freedoms with a recognition of how power, through structures, disciplines, organisations and environments, contributes to the formation of subjectivities. This requires moving on from idealised, humanist accounts of rational individual agency and recognition that construction of the self is not a purely discursive process and is certainly more than a by-product of the types of educational resources an individual chooses to consume.

One important marker of this issue is the absence of discussions of embodiment or situation in work advocating online forms of open education. The participation of learners is curiously rarified. As Dall'Alba and Barnacle argued (2005), the conventional design of programmes involves imparting knowledge and skills in a way that is decontextualized from the practices to which they belong, a problem that they trace back to Cartesian dualism. They proposed countering this phenomenologically, drawing on Merleau-Ponty's ideas of embodied knowing and the extension into and unison with other bodies, entities and things that comprise the world.

This move draws attention to what Land (2005) described as the "incorporeal fallacy" of online learning: the apparent dissipation of human bodies from discussion or consideration. Reacting against this, Land observed that "cyberspace could well be a non-space, but the subjects who inhabit it always remain embodied" (p. 154). Granted, sociotechnical developments can imply "a new, different, and complex way of experiencing the relationship between the physical human body and the 'I' that inhabits it" (Stone, 1991, p. 86). But, as Stone (1991) argued, although we may have learnt to delegate agency to body-representatives that exist in an imaginary space, and while there may have been a trend toward understanding the body as physical and the subject as textual, the body still remains.

Dreyfus (2008) argued that this raises questions for all forms of online education, proposing that "Internet user's disembodiment has profound and unexpected effects" and may undermine the credibility of the endeavour (p. 3). He is perhaps premature in celebrating the force of his arguments, particularly given subsequent developments with MOOCs:

> Most of Chapter Two predicting the failure of disembodied distance learning and ridiculing the enthusiasts who predicted that, thanks to the Internet, an Ivy League education would be available to everyone on the planet and that Universities as we know them would disappear had to be scrapped. It is now clear that distance learning has failed. The major universities have given up on it and consider their investments of hundreds of thousands of dollars sunk costs. (p. xi)

However, it is hard to shake off such concerns, not least because MOOCs have failed to provide the 'avalanche' or revolution higher education was promised; the enthusiasts have not been fully vindicated, either.

An important consideration in Dreyfus's (2008) arguments is what he meant by 'disembodied.' Obviously, he is not proposing the literal absence of the material body; he directly challenges the enthusiasts who aspire to "sloughing off our situated bodies" (p. 50). Instead, as he elaborated, his concern is more with whether "the mediated information concerning distant objects and people transmitted to us over the Internet as telepresence would be as present as anything could get" (p. 54). As an example, he pointed to things like the Mars Sojourner, where the perceptual delays that follow from controlling it emphasise our lack of direct presence.

However, whilst delays in response to control signals may make an operator acutely aware of not being present with the Mars Rover, they probably neither expect nor want a faithful experience of being present on the surface of Mars. Instead, what they have is a sense of presence in the control room of a scientific mission, using a distributed network of scientific tools that include the experimental apparatus of the rover; and this experience of doing scientific work is direct, risky and meaningful in its own right. Even where specialist technology mediates our experience of the object of study, we may still have available to us a direct experience of what it means to study such an object.

The reason this matters is because of student expectations. A student studying online and expecting to experience the same kind of conversation he or she would have in a one-to-one tutorial or a group workshop may well find the mediation of discussions inimical to a sense of presence. However, students expecting to study in isolation, primarily reading texts on screen, may find the experience of chatting to fellow students live on an audio conferencing tool such as Skype, or engaging in complex, closely argued exchanges with their peers in an online discussion forum, far more sociable than they were expecting. If the online exchange is understood as a proxy for the classroom, it will fall short of that benchmark. But if a different benchmark is chosen—specifically, if such online interactions form an expected part of what it means to study, which, for a growing (but not universal) group of people is exactly what they expect (Jones & Healing, 2010)—then this itself is the direct experience that they were looking for.

To elaborate this point, we can draw on Heidegger's distinction between tools that are ready-to-hand and those that are present-at-hand. Tools that are ready-to-hand form part of a network of things and practices, and we use them without having to focus on them to achieve meaningful ends. By contrast, we are aware of those that are present-at-hand—perhaps because they are unfamiliar or broken, or they are hindering the task at hand. Making sense of them involves focusing on them, theorizing them, to mend, master or improve them in some way.

For the operator of the Mars Sojourner, the difficulties of controlling the rover in the face of communication lag, a challenging environment and so on, all suggest that the rover itself might well be present-at-hand, a struggle to control and so a constant reminder of the way presence is mediated. However, in the control room itself, the keyboard and mouse being used to issue commands to the rover might be ready-to-hand; this part of the network is familiar, not an object of focus, and even though the action involves complex, distributed technologies, the controller might experience their presence in the control room as immediate.

To echo this point within an educational context, if an online student tries to use a bulletin board to recreate the experience of chatting about a concept, or an experiment, or a research paper, with one of his or her peers, that student might well find that the use of a virtual learning environment obscures the intended discussion. The student's sense of presence will feel mediated. However, a student caught up in writing an essay, using alt-tab to swap between Microsoft Word and Google Scholar while searching for journal articles to support his or her argument, might well experience a kind of flow state, one in which the student is so focused on the task that he or she is not directly aware of the fluency with which these tools are used. What the student is focused on is writing.

Writing is, and always has been, a technologically mediated activity—a point that can be traced back to Plato's accounts of Socrates's dialogue with Phaedrus. Law (1992) elaborated the networks that writing as communication involves, for example—such as the computer keyboard, the computer, paper, printing presses, the postal system and so on. However, although writing—a central part of almost every educational experience—is always mediated, it seems inappropriate to condemn all writing as 'disembodied' experience.

What this suggests, then, is the important issue is not the pursuit of an unmediated embodiment but a question of using appropriate technologies to engage with the world. Dall'Alba and Barnacle (2005) developed this point in relation to online learning, drawing on Ihde's work to argue that our embodiment is transformed through the extension of the body by sophisticated modern technologies, including the Internet. Adopting such a relational perspective supports a more complex account of the role of technology.

> So while the word processor does indeed transform writing practices, the transformation is not simply an imposition. Rather, the transformation occurs through the mediated relation between "user" and machine, where the parameters and potentials of both are transformed (although not necessarily symmetrically).... The impact of technologies, therefore, is neither singular nor predictable as their performance also reconstitutes our own desires and actions. (Dall'Alba & Barnacle, 2005, p. 735)

As a consequence, they argued, the use of the Internet to support distance learning does not necessarily result in disembodiment and disengagement. Instead, the opportunities it provides for extending the body through technologies can make different kinds of presence and engagement possible; they become the means of inquiry, from the natural sciences through to philosophy (Ihde, 2005). Perhaps more provocatively, where such forms of engagement are part of the hermeneutic process itself, confronting students with unfamiliar technologies, with things that leave them feeling disembodied, which are experienced as present-at-hand, may be a productive thing to do, precisely because it requires them to theorize the technology and to make sense of it as part of specific kinds of being-in-the-world.

Adopting this stance on the relationships between tools and knowledge draws attention back to the specific situations in which learners find themselves and how these play into the success or failure of their studies, requiring us to explain the materiality of social practices (Latour, 2005). Such sociomaterial analyses reveal the tensions between freedom *from* and freedom *to*, outlined earlier.

> The campus—or more generally, the co-location of learners, teachers, labs, classrooms, lecture theatres, libraries and so on—refuses to lie down and die.... Those seeking to develop distributed education should understand the support a campus setting gives the educational process and should be prepared for the necessity to find new ways of providing that support in a distributed education context. (Cornford & Pollock, 2005, p. 170)

Cornford and Pollock (2005) talked about the campus as a 'resourceful constraint,' one that does indeed create problems of geographical access but which is taken up repeatedly and successfully in the academic work of students and staff, day after day, around the world. The material campus provides what Bowker and Star (2000, pp. 34–35) described as an infrastructure: something that is embedded within other social structures; is transparent (in that it supports tasks without being noticed), at least once people become familiar with it; persists across time and/or space; develops in modular increments because it is big, layered and complex, and so on. Attending to the networks of people and things that students rely upon in their studies reveals the consistent presence of infrastructural elements. The sheer volume and persistence of learning practices undertaken in these conventional sites of study is testament to their ongoing value; however, students also study in a range of other settings, including their homes, parks and on public transport (Gourlay & Oliver, 2013). The campus tells an important part of the story but not the entirety of it.

To understand how students are already moving beyond the constraints of the campus, it is useful to draw on a mobilities perspective. Instead of seeing spaces such as a container or backcloth, or from the perspective of open education as some kind of trap or barrier, a mobilities analysis explores how spaces are enacted and become sedimented across time (Edwards, Tracey, & Jordan, 2011). Rather than assuming the function of, say, a 'lecture theatre,' it involves exploring how specific educational practices enacted in that space come to frame it in a way that is consistently recognizable. Following the flows of studying, as people and things move from place to place, it becomes possible to identify 'open' aspects of practices where mobility becomes possible (across time, space and forms of mediation), as well as aspects where practice has instead become tethered. Such tethering is not inherently bad—having infrastructures ready-to-hand allows freedom *to*, rather than having to rebuild the material conditions for knowledge work at each new instance of the practice. Indeed, tethering is necessary: Stability across time is what gives things coherence, and in the case of open education, would allow us to talk about learning as opposed to just a series of momentary experiences. Such tethering need not be in the order of whole programmes of study, of course, but this does need to be considered.

The imperative then becomes finding ways to mobilize infrastructure and to understand the specific kinds of tethering that diverse learners find problematic. It also requires us to appreciate the specific kinds of mobilities that diverse learners find problematic, since the work required to reconnect material environments to knowledge practices can be considerable. Students persist in the face of remarkable challenges, as demonstrated, for example, by the way in which students in South Africa persisted with online courses using cell phones, to overcome the infrastructural challenges of unreliable power supplies and Internet connections (Czerniewicz, Williams, & Brown, 2009). It is striking that, "in these difficult conditions, so seriously constraining in real ways, some students are able to overcome structural challenges which would seem to determine their actions" (Czerniewicz et al., 2009, p. 81). Part of the explanation of this rests on the way in which these individuals had tethered particular learning practices to their phone, allowing them to substitute this relatively reliable infrastructure as a point of stability and continuity in their ongoing studies, replacing other more erratic and unreliable infrastructures. However, it is important to note that these replacements were things that the students had to assemble themselves: Even where the material infrastructure (the phone, the cell network) was already in place, these had to be enrolled into the service of learning, requiring the development of new connections (from the phone to the virtual learning environment, the phone screen to PDFs, etc.) and new practices (participating via the phone in online discussions, reading academic papers on very small screens). New forms of openness had been achieved, but students paid a price in terms of the effort and cost of making studying possible.

CONCLUSIONS

The open education movement strives to achieve important moral ends, envisaging a more participative, inclusive form of education for the future. However, the way in which this is pursued is often simplistic. Considerable attention is given to the removal of barriers, to achieving freedom *from* constraints on learning. The question of what learners might then be free *to* do is less attended to. Removing barriers is an important part of the whole process of opening education, but it is only part of what is needed.

This simplistic view is enabled by conceptions of learning that treat learners as nodes or components in an information system. By disregarding the complexities of embodied, situated experience, learning becomes a more tractable problem. If these complexities are brought back into the discussion, questions arise as to how learners can construct the complex sociomaterial networks they need to learn. It also highlights that learners' experiences will be diverse, being influenced by the wide range of contexts that they create or find themselves in, and also that these will necessarily vary over time.

One way in which the open education can respond to this is by attending to the ways in which specific groups manage to mobilise their learning. To be coherent, learning needs points of stability and continuity—these might be provided by institutions but can also be associated with devices, people or other spaces. Rather than vilifying universities, which have developed to provide incredibly successful and persistent sites of tethering, it might be possible to learn from these successes. Where equally successful points of tethering could be created that were (for example) associated with devices rather than spaces, this might well open education up in important new ways—although it must be recognized that this comes at a price, with geographical freedom traded off against the economic costs of acquiring and maintaining the device. Achieving a greater degree of openness in one arena requires a greater degree of closure in another.

Arguably, then, no form of education can become completely free without losing all coherence and recognisability. However, it is possible and important to create a broader repertoire of *kinds* of freedom. Achieving this may help create forms of open education appropriate for the diverse needs of the wide array of learners that all of us want to help.

REFERENCES

Atkins, D., Brown J., & Hammond A. (2007). *A review of the Open Educational Resources (OER) movement: Achievements, challenges, and new opportunities*. Menlo Park, Ca.: The William and Flora Hewlett Foundation. http://www.hewlett.org/uploads/files/ReviewoftheOERMovement.pdf

Barber, M., Donnelly, K., & Rizvi, S. (2013, March). An avalanche is coming: Higher education and the revolution ahead. *Institute for Public Policy Research*. London, UK: Institute for Public Policy Research. Retrieved from http://med.stanford.edu/smili/support/FINAL%20Avalanche%20Paper%20110313%20(2).pdf

Biesta, G. (2012). Giving teaching back to education: Responding to the disappearance of the teacher. *Phenomenology & Practice, 6*(2), 35–49.

Bowker, G. C., & Star, S. L. (2000). *Sorting things out: Classification and its consequences*. Cambridge, MA: The MIT press.

Caswell, T., Henson, S., Jensen, M., & Wiley, D. (2008, February). Open educational resources: Enabling universal education. *The International Review of Research in Open and Distance Learning*, *9*(1), 1–11. Retrieved from http://www.irrodl.org/index.php/irrodl/article/view/469/1009

Cornford, J., & Pollock, N. (2005). The university campus as a "resourceful constraint": Process and practice in the construction of the virtual university. In M. Lea & K. Nicoll (Eds.), *Distributed learning: Social and cultural approaches to practice* (pp. 170–181). London, UK: RoutledgeFalmer.

Czerniewicz, L., Williams, K., & Brown, C. (2009). Students make a plan: understanding student agency in constraining conditions. *Research in Learning Technology*, *17*(2), 75–88.

Dall'Alba, G., & Barnacle, R. (2005). Embodied knowing in online environments. *Educational Philosophy and Theory*, *37*(5), 719–744.

Downes, S. (2011). Free learning: Essays on open educational resources and copyright. *National Research Council Canada*. Retrieved from http://www.downes.ca/files/books/FreeLearning.pdf

Dreyfus, H. (2008). *On the internet*. London, UK: Routledge.

Edwards, R. (1997). *Changing places? Flexibility, lifelong learning, and a learning society*. New York, NY: Psychology Press.

Edwards, R., Tracey, F. & Jordan, K. (2011). Mobilities, moorings and boundary marking in developing semantic technologies in educational practices. *Research in Learning Technology*, *19*(3), 219–232.

Friedman, T. (2013, January 26). Revolution hits the universities. *The New York Times*. Retrieved from http://www.nytimes.com/2013/01/27/opinion/sunday/friedman-revolution-hits-the-universities.html

Friesen, N. (2010). Ethics and the technologies of empire: E-learning and the US military. *AI & Society*, *25*(1), 71–81.

Gourlay, L., & Oliver, M. (2013). Beyond "the social": Digital literacies as sociomaterial practice. In R. Goodfellow & M. Lea (Eds.), *Literacy in the digital university: Critical perspectives on learning, scholarship and technology* (pp. 79–94). London, UK: Routledge.

Ihde, D. (2005). More material hermeneutics. In A. Bammé, G. Getzinger & B. Wieser (Ed). *In Yearbook of the Institute for Advanced Studies on Science, Technology and Society* (pp. 341–350). Munich, Germany: Profil Verlag.

Jones, C., & Healing, G. (2010). Net generation students: Agency and choice and the new technologies. *Journal of Computer Assisted Learning*, *26*(5), 344–356.

Knox, J. (2013). Five critiques of the open educational resources movement. *Teaching in Higher Education*, *18*(8), 821–832.

Land, R. (2005). Embodiment and risk in cyberspace education. In R. Land & S. Bayne (Eds.), *Education in cyberspace* (pp. 149–164). London, UK: Routledge.

Lane, A. (2008). Widening participation in education through open educational resources. In T. Iiyoshi & M. S. Vijay Kumar (Eds.), *Opening up education: The collective advancement of education through open technology, open content, and open knowledge* (pp. 149–163). Cambridge, MA: The MIT Press.

Latour, B. (2005). *Reassembling the social*. Oxford, UK: Oxford University Press.

Laurillard, D. (2008). Open teaching: The key to sustainable and effective open education. In T. Iiyoshi & M. S. Vijay Kumar (Eds.), *Opening up education: The collective advancement of education through open technology, open content, and open knowledge* (pp. 319–335). Cambridge, MA: The MIT Press.

Law, J. (1992). Notes on the theory of the actor-network: Ordering, strategy and heterogeneity. *Systems Practice*, *5*, 379–393.

Lewin, T. (2012, March 4). Instruction for masses knocks down campus walls. *The New York Times.* Retrieved from http://www.nytimes.com/2012/03/05/education/moocs-large-courses-open-to-all-topple-campus-walls.html?_r=0

Mackie, J. (2008). Open source in open education: Promises and challenges. In T. Iiyoshi & M. S. Vijay Kumar (Eds.), *Opening up education: The collective advancement of education through open technology, open content, and open knowledge* (pp. 119–132). Cambridge, MA: The MIT Press.

Mayes, J. T. (1995). Learning technology and Groundhog Day. In W. Strang, V. B. Simpson, & D. Slater (Eds.), *Hypermedia at work: Practice and theory in higher education* (pp. 21–37). Canterbury, UK: University of Kent Press.

McAuley, A., Stewart, B., Siemens, G., & Cormier, D. (2010). *The MOOC model for digital practice.* Retrieved from https://www.academia.edu/2857149/The_MOOC_model_for_digital_practice

Peter, S., & Deimann, M. (2013). On the role of openness in education: A historical reconstruction. *Open Praxis, 5*(1), 7–14.

Ross, J., Sinclair, C., Knox, J., Bayne, S., & Macleod, H. (2014). Teacher experiences and academic identity: The missing components of MOOC pedagogy. *Journal of Online Learning and Teaching, 10*(1), 57–69.

Stone, A. (1991). Will the real body please stand up? In M. Benedikt (Ed.), *Cyberspace: First steps* (pp. 81–118). Cambridge, MA: The MIT Press.

Taylor, J. C. (2007). Open courseware futures: Creating a parallel universe. *e-Journal of Instructional Science and Technology, 10*(1), 1–9. Retrieved from http://ascilite.org/archived-journals/e-jist/docs/vol10_no1/papers/full_papers/taylorj.pdf

Weller, M. (2014). *The battle for open: How openness won and why it doesn't feel like victory.* London, UK: Ubiquity Press.

CHAPTER NINE

Open Learning AND Social Innovation: Freedom AND Democratic Culture

MICHAEL A. PETERS, RICHARD HERAUD AND ANDREW GIBBONS

With the advent of the Internet, principles of openness have become the basis of innovative institutional forms that decentralize and democratize power relationships, promote access to knowledge and encourage symmetrical, horizontal peer learning relationships. New "peer philosophies" are at the heart of a notion of "openness" that rest on the historical significance of peer governance, peer review, peer learning and peer collaboration as a collection of nested and emergent values that form the basis for open institutions and open management philosophies (Peters, 2012). These in turn offer significant implications for localised and individual empowerment, where learners can work together using effective pedagogies to meet the needs of their communities.

In this chapter we explore the 'links' between openness and innovation through the philosophy of peer learning and forms of 'creative labour': collective intelligence, crowdsourcing, social collaboration and the educational web science of the social mind—embodied, embedded, extended and enacted. The first section provides a view of the changing global digital economy, focusing on *open education* as a movement comprised of digital "knowledge cultures" (Peters & Besley, 2006) that build on overlapping and nested convergences of open source, open data, open access, open publishing and open governance movements. The chapter relates this movement to the concept of 'openness' and its underlying political values, as well as forward in terms of analysis of the present historical moment, the "*reconstitution of the social*" (Peters, 2012), characterizing the emerging paradigm of 'social media' and 'social production.'

The chapter explores the complexity of the shift from mediation and production to innovation and how social innovation produces new possibilities of freedom and democracy. The networked community, whether this be in education or in the proprietary domain, supposes the formalization of new possibilities for collective engagement and, as such, as Pierre Lévy has been arguing since the 1990s, collective intelligence. This latter project enables the collaboration of more recent research with the intention of trying to understand the manner in which the global networked information economy changes the nature of public goods. This new experience of freedom and democracy is not regarded as merely an interesting outcome of this process but rather comprises the conditions under which collective intelligence is understood to emerge. Rather than technology being something to be feared, it is offering, as Lévy highlighted (as cited in Peters, 2015a), new possibilities, of which the concept of 'We-Think' (Leadbeater, 2008) is but one example. The purpose of this exploration is to theoretically develop some of the significant themes that are coming to characterize our reflection on the relationship among open learning, social innovation, freedom and democracy.

OPEN EDUCATION AND SOCIAL PRODUCTION OF KNOWLEDGE

Open publishing, open access and open data can be considered parts of a wider movement called *open education* that builds on the nested and evolving convergences of open source, open access and open science and also is emblematic of a set of still wider political and economic changes that ushers in "social production" as an aspect of the global digital economy, an economy that is both fragile and volatile, as the current world credit and banking crisis demonstrates.

This decade can be called the "open" decade (open source, open systems, open standards, open archives, open everything), just as the decade of the 1990s was called the "electronic" decade (e-text, e-learning, e-commerce, e-governance; Materu, 2004). And yet it is more than just a "decade" that follows the electronic innovations of the 1990s; it is a change of philosophy and ethos, a set of interrelated and complex changes that transforms markets and the mode of production, ushering in a new collection of values based on openness, the ethic of participation and peer-to-peer collaboration.

These transformations have opened up "new ways of thinking about education, and about the future of education in an era that seems bound to become incessantly more digitized" (Loveless & Williamson, 2013, p. 1).

> Emerging devices and technologies like track-and-trace technologies, digital mapping, software visualization, transactional data, data mining, social network analysis, digital databases, wikis, Web 2.0 and open source social analytics are all beginning to change the ways in which learning can be tracked, recorded, visualized, patterned, documented and presented. Digitally networked learning is being inseparably shaped through new transactional methods that are genealogically rooted in commercial interests and non-humanist transactional politics. These are implications as yet little explored. (Loveless & Williamson, 2013, p. 34)

However emergent open education might appear, this 'openness' can be grouped around a successive series of utopian historical moments based on a set of similar ideas stemming from core Enlightenment concepts of freedom, equality, democracy and creativity (Peters, 2009).

The early history of open education consists of both political and psychological experiments based on extending the concept of freedom that were conducted in special/alternative schools established in the early 20th century. The movement from the very beginning thus was shaped by contemporary political and psychological theory that attempted to provide alternatives to the mainstream and was connected to and exemplified a form of society and set of institutions that were seen as politically desirable. This was in effect seen as the opportunity to engineer a social democratic society through education.

These early ideas significantly involved an analysis of the space and architecture of schools and the associated idea of freedom of movement. The 20th century saw considerable refinement and development of the physical properties of the institution, which filtered into "mainstream" thinking and practice in moderate, if largely insufficient and unsuccessful, experimentation—for instance, the 'open plan classroom' of the 1970s. An important aspect concerned not only the analysis of architecture and its constraining effects on learning but the overcoming of distance in a form of distance education that began in the late 19th century through correspondence and progressed through various media, including that of radio and television.

Open education consisted of several strands and movements that often coalesced and overlapped to create a complex historical skein that, despite the complexity, was poised to rapidly avail itself of new communication and information technologies in the last decade of the 20th century and to identify itself more broadly with the new convergences among open source, open access and open courseware movements. It was as though the open education movement in its infancy required the technological infrastructure to emerge as a major new paradigm rather than a set of small-scale and experimental alternatives or a form of distance education. These utopian moments can be described and analysed as five historical moments involving the development of the *open classroom,* the advent and experiment of *open schooling,* the establishment of the *open university,* the development of *open access* and *open courseware* and the eventual emergence of a fully fledged notion and practice of *open education*. The movements have each contributed to the collaborative, ground-up, theorisation and practice of teaching and learning. Continuing experimentation around distributed knowledge and learning systems takes these movements into a phase of *open learning systems*. These systems are designed as a contemporary digital solution to the school textbook and attempt to manage five interrelated problems:

1. The problem of *excess information* and the selection of content.
2. The problem of *information validation* and the development of appropriate critical attitudes and standards of recognition of sources.
3. The problem of *the diversity of forms* of new media, which include traditional print media but also digital photographs, artefacts, web sites and embedded videos.
4. The problem of *the development of user-content creation* by teachers and students (coproduction of knowledge) within state curriculum frameworks that outline topics, definitions, concepts, principles, content areas and questions.
5. *The problem of attention* with the traditional school textbook, that is, attractiveness of the text is 'sad' compared with the students' experience of modern media, which is interactive, dynamic and current (continuously updated).

Open education then embodies three main aspects that draw from the movements noted earlier: openness of learning content (full courses, courseware and journals), tools for openness (software to support the development, use, reuse and delivery of learning content and management systems) and implementation of openness (through intellectual property licences to promote open publishing and design principles of best practice with localized content; OECD, 2007). Open education in the broader sense also connects and overlaps with new digital technologies that reconfigure open publishing, including changes in the distribution and consumption of information. For example, the Ithaka Report, "University Publishing in a Digital Age" (Brown, Griffiths & Rascoff, 2007), emphasized the following:

> **Changes in creation, production and consumption of scholarly resources**—creation of new formats made possible by digital technologies, ultimately allowing scholars to work in deeply integrated electronic research and publishing environments that will enable real-time dissemination, collaboration, dynamically-updated content, and usage of new media. (p. 4)
>
> **Alternative distribution models** (institutional repositories, pre-print servers, open access journals) have also arisen with the aim to broaden access, reduce costs, and enable open sharing of content. (p. 4)

Emboldened by these new digital technologies and the changes they make possible, groups of scholars have come out in favour of the open education model. For instance, the Cape Town Open Education Declaration of 2007 indicated that we are on the cusp of a global revolution in teaching and learning, where educators worldwide are developing a vast pool of educational resources on the Internet, open and free for all to use.[1] Open education builds on the nested and evolving convergences of open source, open access and open science and also is emblematic of a set of still wider political and economic changes that ushered in 'social production' (and, as explored next, 'social innovation') as an aspect of the global digital economy.

NETWORKED INFORMATION ECONOMIES

In *The Wealth of Networks: How Social Production Transforms Markets and Freedom*, Benkler (2006) developed a vision of the good society based on access and distribution of information goods in a networked global information economy that places a high value on individual autonomy. Benkler's work links to a broader tradition of thinkers who have attempted to retheorize the public domain, such as Jane Jacobs, James Scott, Richard Sennett and Iris Marion Young. Within the public information space of the Internet and the information commons, people have the individual means to pursue their own interests. The emergence of the global networked information economy, made possible by increasingly cheaper processors linked as a pervasive network, has created an information economy based on the production of information and culture that enables social and nonmarket or peer-to-peer production and exchange to play a, perhaps even the, central role.

The environment of the networked information economy is an ambiguous domain in that the value of knowledge can be interpreted in ways that fundamentally change the nature of the learning domain. For example, if this domain were described in the way that Lévy (1997) described "the commodity space" (pp. 135–138), then knowledge comes to be ascribed with a commercial value though being regarded as something that can be consumed and/or produced.

On the other hand, if knowledge is ascribed a value that supposes a capacity to contribute to the development of "human qualities" (Lévy, 1997, p. 140), then the networked information economy is no longer merely a received domain: It is a metaphor for what the contents of the domain refer to and, as such, it becomes an invitation to transform those contents. In this way, the metaphor itself is transformed. Autonomy created in this domain occurs, in Lévy's (1997) words, through the enhancement of intelligence, the coordination of intelligence in real-time and effective application of skills. It is through these actions that Lévy understands human qualities to be developed as a consequence of individual engagement in the networked economy. Understood in its most optimistic form, this ideal symbolizes an opportunity to develop human qualities through creative coproduction.

While these two models of the learning space—the commodity space and the knowledge space—are conceptually very different from the point of view of understanding the nature of the distinctive opportunities they offer, the learning experience of the student is one that potentially engages both spaces simultaneously, the commodity space sitting inside the knowledge space, as it were. In these circumstances, the distinction between the proprietary and the nonproprietary is not determined by the power of these spaces to prescribe actions of a particular nature—decision as consumer, for example—but by the actions being understood as a response to an opportunity to transform the received reality. The knowledge space hence involves a constant production of new metaphoric understanding of that which the individual engages with and hence involves a constant refinement of the experience of autonomy.

As Benkler (2006) put it, "[p]eer-production projects often are composed of people who want to do something in the world and turn to the network to find a community of peers willing to work together to make that wish a reality" (p. 137). This mutual desire is not implicit to the function of the networked information economy when it is understood as a commodity space. In the second model, each individual decides

> ...[t]o take advantage of some combination of technical, organizational, and social within which we have come to live, and to become an active creator of his or her world, rather than merely to accept what was already there. The belief that it is possible to make something valuable happen in the world, and the practice of actually acting on that belief, represent a qualitative improvement in the condition of individual freedom. They mark the emergence of new practices of self-directed agency as a lived experience, going beyond mere formal permissibility and theoretical possibility. (Benkler, 2006, p. 137)

Charles Leadbeater (2008) characterized these shifts as a form of We-Think and emphasized the move from mass production to mass innovation characterized by self-help and self-organization. These practices reorient traditions of community development in terms of collective self-organization that demonstrates the shifts from mass consumption to mass participation. The emphasis is on mass creativity, distributed networked organization and a new ethic of collaboration. Leadbeater (2008) drew attention to the social production of media in examples of Wikipedia, YouTube and new business models of Google, Yahoo, Microsoft and Amazon that represent the end of the value chain and new forms of networked value based on distributed means of media production and ownership with shared infrastructure, shared platforms and the commons. He argued that these new media communities encourage participative media and new freedoms. Social media encourages a sense of personal autonomy that enables a democracy based on values such as self-organisation, free association and self-regulation. The rise of social, commons-based media production allows us to imagine how we could reorganise ourselves, promoting greater freedom, democracy and justice, while also promoting innovation and efficiency (Leadbeater, 2008).

Although it has more distant philosophical origins, 'I-Think' might be thought of as a product of the industrial economy in the sense that it is in this paradigm that it realizes its ultimate form. In industrial society, mankind is 'massified' as a consumer community while at the same time idealizing the autonomous chooser. The mechanism by which the individual's experience of freedom makes him or her a distinctive entity in the marketplace has to do with how personal choice is intrinsically bound to an ascribed notion of personal responsibility. This autonomous chooser is both theorized and critiqued as if this individual should be a logical and self-subjugating product of the Cartesian *cogito, ergo sum*, "I think, therefore I am" (Leadbeater, 2008, p. 19).[2]

If the networked information economy were to be thought of as "the knowledge space" (Lévy, 1997, pp. 138–141), in the manner referred to earlier, "self-organization and sociability" will result in the production of "subjectivities" (Lévy, 1997, p. 141) expressed in the form of new "human qualities." The identity of the individual associated with the production of capital goods, in "the commodity space," can no longer be theorized as such when this individual becomes productive in "the knowledge space." Identification with "a category, trade, or community" (Lévy, 1997, p. 3), such as the working class or the trade of being a builder, causes a minority culture to give way to the formation of the subjectivities that transcend the use of such identities. As Lévy (1997) and Benkler (2006) suggested, the autonomy of the individual in these circumstances is strengthened. How then are we to think of this strengthening of the individual autonomy such that it might be thought to enhance 'collective intelligence' (Lévy, 1997) through a process of We-Think (Leadbeater, 2008) and without succumbing to identifying ourselves as actors who can only be described by the roles ascribed by the industrial economy?

This is not an easy question to answer in that the knowledge space is only in an early stage of its development (Peters, 2015a), and much depends on what new knowledge might emerge during the development of collective intelligence. At this stage, it is possible to say that the knowledge space is "a space in which the processes of individual and collective subjectivization come together" (Lévy, 1997, p. 139), a space in which it might be presumed that individuals constitute their diversity of experience in relation to distinctive but complementary human qualities.

In light of this discussion, how are we to contemplate the dynamic of We-Think in the networked information economy? Leadbeater (2008) asked two questions: (a) "[W]hy do some collaborations turn into We-Think—seemingly generating a momentum and intelligence of its own—while others do not?" and, (b) "How do creative communities avoid becoming inward-looking cliques that ignore new ideas brought [in] by outsiders?" (p. 61). According to Leadbeater, these basic organizational questions must be effectively addressed if We-Think is to emerge.

Leadbeater (2008) identified five actions: "core," "contribute," "connect," "collaborate" and "create" (pp. 68–83). "Innovative communities invariably start with a gift of knowledge provided by someone" (p. 68), where "innovation comes from a creative conversation between people who combine their different skills, insights and knowledge to explore a problem" (Lester & Piore, 2004, as cited in Leadbeater, 2008, p. 69). "A good core [or five to seven individuals] starts a conversation and invites other people to contribute" (Leadbeater, 2008, p. 69).

This articulation of the concept of We-Think highlights both the *social* and *open* aspects of it: It is *social* in the form of a conversation involving individuals who work cohesively on account of sharing an interest in a common problem, and it is *open* in the manner in which the concept of the problem is implicitly understood to contain an invitation to invite new contributors, who it is believed will bring new, diverse and challenging perspectives on how the problem itself might be understood and addressed. We-Think is, as Leadbeater acknowledged (2008), a form of open innovation. But can we also say that We-Think is a form of social innovation just because the process of open innovation has a social aspect? It would seem easy to presume that both open innovation and social innovation are intrinsically connected for the simple reason that all innovation is now thought of as being collective (Leadbeater, 2008). This notion of the relationship between open innovation and social innovation pays no regard to the social problem that social innovation might pretend to address in the thinking of other theorists (see, e.g., Mulgan, 2013; Unger, 2013). For this reason, it would seem appropriate to look more closely at how Leadbeater understands the concept and practice of innovation *per se*.[3]

Leadbeater (2008) promoted We-Think as an alternative model to the so-called invention-driven "pipeline model of innovation" (p. 92). We-Think, as a model of open innovation, "uses the web to take to scale a collaborative and social approach to creativity" (p. 93). However, it is tempting to ask whether We-Think is really both innovation and creativity and not 'just' creativity. To Leadbeater, innovation would appear to be best described as a creative conversation that blends ideas. Leadbeater seems to favour the idea that the role of new ideas is to contribute to incremental innovative activity, where innovation is promoted through diffusion with the intention of consolidating the function of the managed economy through creating greater efficiency. The formative nature of We-Think suggests that there is interesting work to be done in the area of how we understand the relationship between invention and opportunity in the networked information economy and furthermore how the relationship of risk to responsibility is mediated through the practical process of forming this relationship.

While they have clear economic benefits in terms of competition, we wish to focus on the political forms that increasingly replace older mass media and also enhance social democratic participation and activism aimed at the protection of freedom of speech and the assertion of rights for the Internet era.

FROM SOCIAL PRODUCTION TO SOCIAL INNOVATION IN THE CULTURE OF OPENNESS

In this section we shift the focus from production to innovation and explore the interconnections of theorising around openness and innovation that establish current trends and trajectories and their driving assumptions and principles.

One of the fundamental insights springing from Steven Weber's (2004) *The Success of Open Source* is the idea that property in open source is configured around the right to distribute, not the right to exclude. An economic system can be built around a core notion of property rights as distribution. It has the potential to become "a political economy and production system process, enabled by the Internet, that makes possible voluntary, distributed innovation and collective creation of complex public goods with neither the bureaucratic structure of the firm as we know it or the financial incentives of the market as we know them."

The Cooperation Commons explained:

> The Internet and a decentralized means of social organization around a production goal make possible "distributed innovation" that radically reduces both transaction and coordination costs, making possible the collective creation of public goods. Although open source software production is the most successful example of this process, it is not the only one. Self-interest combines with a norm of sharing a public good that benefits all; learning, reputation capital, and solving a problem one already needs to solve ("scratching an itch") are individual motivating factors. Self-election eliminates the cost of hierarchical management—individuals decide what to work on. Free-riders contribute to positive network effects by increasing the size of the user base, and aggregate infinitesmal contributions into significant efficiency gains by occasionally reporting a rare bug or complaining about a missing feature. (see http://www.cooperationcommons.com/node/411)

Generalizable characteristics of open source process, characteristics that lend to user-driven innovation, are identified by the Cooperation Commons as including the following:

- The GPL (General Public License) uses copyright law to configure property around the right to distribute rather than the right to exclude.
- The GPL creates a system of value creation and a set of governance mechanisms that enable the distributed production, maintenance, and development of highly complex software code.

- The open source community's organizing principles include "criteria for entering and leaving, leadership roles, power relations, distributional issues, education and socialization paths, and all the other characteristics that describe a nascent culture and community structure."
- User-driven innovation takes place in a parallel distributed setting, distinct forms and mechanisms of cooperative behavior regulated by norms and governance structures, and the economic logic of "antirival" goods that recasts the "problem" of free riding.
- "The key element of the open source process, as an ideal type, is voluntary participation and voluntary selection of tasks." Coordination costs are dramatically lowered by self-election: each contributor chooses what to work on, when to start, and when to quit.
- Eight general principles that capture the essence of what people do in the open source process: Make it interesting and make sure it happens; scratch an itch (link private contributions to a public good); minimize how many times you have to reinvent the wheel; solve problems through parallel work processes whenever possible; leverage the law of large numbers; document what you do; release early and release often; talk a lot.
- Open source production is social because it is a product of voluntary collective collaboration, political because structures and organizations allocate resources and manage conflicts, technical because the final product is software code that must work, and economic in a fundamental sense of understanding the way individual choices about what to do with limited time and energy aggregate to a macro-level.
- Four organizational principles needed for distributed innovation: "Empower people to experiment. Enable bits of information to find each other. Structure information so it can recombine with other pieces of information. Create a governance system that sustains this process."
(For the full list, see http://www.cooperationcommons.com/node/411)[4]

These elements of production and distribution have, over a decade, come to define an epochal period of "transition bridging two very different types of economies and cultures" (Bollier, 2006, p. 5). A transition from a 'push' to a 'pull' economy shifts thinking from attempts to either anticipate or determine consumer demand to accumulating and sharing knowledge of consumer demand to produce products customised for local needs. Flexible networks are key to the production process in a pull economy, replacing "standardized distribution channels and marketing" (Bollier, 2006, p. 6) that required systems of mass production of homogenous goods.

Attention to social innovation occurs in a pull economy with the recognition and valuing of a diversity of opinions. An individual's private, independent opinions may be unreliable/inaccurate; however, when taken as contributing to collective wisdom, they can be valued for their generative properties. In a pull economy, a diversity of opinions and specialised and localised knowledges are connected into knowledge sharing networks—in other words mechanisms for the open sharing of knowledge are critical, hence the technological requirements of social innovation. However, as noted elsewhere, technological innovation is not the focus or the purpose but rather the new and open connections that are made possible.

Chesbrough (2003, 2006) and Chesbrough, Vanhaverbeke, and West (2006) explored these connections in terms of principles of open and closed innovation. They argued that open innovation needs a different mind-set and company culture than that used in traditional or closed innovation. A closed mind-set and culture are thought to inhibit the innovation process through the securing and siloing of individuals and groups in processes oriented toward research and development for the sole benefit of the institution.

In open innovation, institutions look elsewhere for ideas and practices and actively encourage multidirectional flows of knowledge with which to join/contribute their own work; institutional cooperation, supported by careful business models, generates sustainable business success/profit.

These shifts in thinking about innovation in social terms put new political emphasis on democratising relationships of production and innovation. For instance, Eric von Hippel (2005) explored the democratising of innovation from the perspective of the consumer. He argued that both institutions and individuals as consumers/users are "increasingly able to innovate for themselves" (p. 1). Von Hippel's analysis of the shift from producer- to consumer-driven innovation argues for significant benefits for the user. In part we might argue that this is because there is no longer the idea of the 'end' user, but that, as von Hippel noted, "individual users do not have to develop everything they need on their own: they can benefit from innovations developed and freely shared by others" (p. 1).

Social innovation, following Scott Page's (2007) work in *The Difference*, is about how groups think and how collective wisdom exceeds the sum of its parts. Innovation requires group decisions and predictions that draw on the unique qualities of individuals—qualities that are limited when isolated.

Page's theory builds on the observation that individuals have distinct tools and abilities. He starts from basic arguments about *heuristics*—mental tools or rules of thumb for dealing with complex situations—and *perspectives*, basic mappings of reality. Given a perspective, a heuristic tells individuals how to search for a solution or to identify an appropriate action; some are simple rules of thumb; others, such as simulated annealing, are more sophisticated. Individuals can also have different *interpretations*, which allow them to lump things together into categories by highlighting one dimension and ignoring others in ways that exploit underlying structures of some kind. Finally, *predictive models* are interpretations which provide a prediction for each set or category created by the interpretation.

This framework allows Page to argue that individuals will build from their perspectives and interpretations toward quite different predictive models. When individuals have different perspectives and/or interpretations, and when they communicate with each other, they are obviously likely to arrive at better solutions than they might in isolation from each other. Different interpretations allow individuals to highlight different aspects of their situations, making them less likely to get stuck at inefficient local optima.

These analyses of 'innovation relationships,' governed by new forms of communication and mediation, by principles of openness and by a radical rethinking of producer-producer, producer-consumer and consumer-consumer relationships, carry a number of interesting implications for education that we explore in the final two sections, beginning with attention to a broader culture of openness.

FREEDOM AS A CONDITION OF THE CULTURE OF OPENNESS

The observations of epochal shifts, these changes in thinking about innovation, represent the continuation of a metastory, albeit in a new register, of freedom. In *Building Knowledge Cultures: Education and Development in the Age of Knowledge Capitalism* Peters and Besley (2006) argued the following:

> There has been a shift from an underlying metaphysics of production—a "productionist" metaphysics—to a metaphysics of consumption and we must now come to understand the new logics and different patterns of cultural consumption in the areas of new media where symbolic analysis becomes a habitual and daily activity. Here the interlocking sets of enhanced mobility of capital, services, and ideas, and the new logics of consumption become all important. These new communicational practices and cross-border flows cannot be effectively policed. More provocatively we might argue, the global informational commons is an emerging infrastructure for the emergence of a civil society still yet unborn.

A new logic of consumption is linked to a classical concept of freedom. Information is the vital element in a 'new' politics and economy that links space, knowledge and capital in networked practices. Freedom is an essential ingredient in this equation if these network practices develop or transform themselves into knowledge cultures. The specific politics and eco-cybernetic rationalities that accompany an informational global capitalism comprised of new multinational edutainment agglomerations are clearly capable of colonizing the emergent ecology of info-social networks and preventing the development of knowledge cultures based on nonproprietary modes of knowledge production and exchange.

The liberal story of education succinctly stated by Kant (1959) in "What is Enlightenment?" as "Dare to think for yourself!" where thinking is equated with 'public reason' and its expression, highlights the troubled history of the relation between education considered as a right and the right to freedom of speech—actually, where the former historically grows out of the other. Here McAfee's (2009) analysis of democracy evident in public decision making draws the debates around Kant's answer to the question back to the domain of process. Following McAfee, where dynamic and generative networks and flows of information occur, flows that are emblematic of new forms of social innovation and establish the conditions of knowledge production, sharing and access, these procedural experiences establish the conditions of openness (and more so than any outcomes decided).

The justification of freedom of speech as a *right* today is associated with eight main lines of argument:

1. Free speech promotes the free exchange of ideas essential to political democracy and its institutions, especially as embodied in the institution of a 'free press' with its new open formats.
2. Free speech promotes the flow of ideas and diversity necessary for innovation and the marketplace, especially in the new mix between public architectures and infrastructures on the one hand and the large scale of the info-utilities on the other.
3. Free speech depends on, but is not limited to, the search for truth and truth as a basis for a community of inquiry.
4. Free speech is also a significant personal, psychological and educational good that promotes the quality of self-expression and thereby the autonomy and development of self, impinging on questions of self-representation and identity.
5. Free speech is a fundamental right that is the hub for a range of academic rights, including the right to learn, the right to access knowledge and information, the right to receive a basic education, and the right to publish.
6. Free speech provides a limit to the ability of the state to subvert other rights and freedoms.
7. Free speech in ancient Greek (παρρησία) is associated with parrheisa, regarded as a fundamental element of democracy in classical Athens, based on the freedom to say (almost) anything, and it also appears in the Midrashic literature connoting open and public communication, analogous to the commons or the public domain (see Foucault, 1983).
8. Free speech associated with digital rights has been theorised and legislated for in terms of Internet rights and principles (Peters, 2012).

Ultimately, these justifications firmly relate questions of the self and self-governance to questions of democratic government, the search for truth (or truth as a regulative ideal) and personal autonomy. While they suggest that there are overriding reasons for accepting that free speech is a basic political principle, they also imply that free speech is not an absolute concept but "limited because it always takes place within a context of competing values" (Mill, 2002). The modern discussion of free speech from John Milton and John Stuart Mill have drawn attention to limiting conditions expressed as principles, such as Mill's principle of harm or Joel Feinberg's principle of offense, especially where it can be demonstrated that so limiting free speech prevents damage to other rights.

Freedom of speech in liberal society exists in a tight network or ecology of rights and constraints that limit it. Momigliano (2003) commented as follows:

> The modern notion of freedom of speech is assumed to include the right of speech in the governing bodies and the right to petition them, the right to relate and publish debates of these bodies, freedom of public meeting, freedom of correspondence, of teaching, of worship, of publishing newspapers and books. Correspondingly, abuse of freedom of speech includes libel, slander, obscenity, blasphemy, sedition.

Furthermore, in a culture of openness, procedure must take into account the ways in which the system approaches the notions of consensus and difference. Sunstein argued for the role of free and open dissent due to his concerns regarding the risks of consensus. Social innovation provides an approach to limiting or removing structures that prohibit the freedom of speech and encouraging the proliferation of the sharing of ideas.

CONCLUSION: SOCIAL INNOVATION, FREEDOM AND EDUCATION

The work of Lev Vygotsky provides a critical and as yet underdeveloped connection between the theorisation of social innovation and the structures and processes of education. While Vygotsky's work has been liberally applied to questions concerning pedagogy, andragogy, and more recently heutagogy, educational policy making and institutional governance appear to be uncertain, at best, as to the systemic conditions of a culture of openness and social innovation as a condition of educational freedom.

Vygotsky's interest in tools, taken up by Jerome Bruner, returns us to the relationship between technological and social innovation that points toward digital agendas for networked and open learning societies:

> With the overall vision of connected learning, new methods of learning based on peer-to-peer distributed systems of collaborative work, open source and mobile networks, de-centred pedagogies, and self-driven learning have been articulated as characteristic of the new network-based age.... In such visions, networks themselves are recast as ideal-typical learning institutions. There is a seemingly natural affinity between networks and the ways in which learning ideally takes place—a highly symbiotic, praxeomorphic form of thinking which understands the psychological aspects of learning as essentially networked, and the mind of the learner as itself a network connected to networks. (Loveless & Williamson, 2013, p. 52)

The open network leads us further and further from the idea of the distinct and self-contained learner. The politics of networked learning challenges perceived centralization and exploitation of innovation through the connection of a new kind of learner:

> The new identity of the learner is to be made up and organized in a pedagogy of connection-making and collective intelligence, through a curriculum that is imagined as a dense web of connections between knowledges, epistemologies, and media, within an ecology of learning in which schools are not centres of education but networked nodes of learning among many other formal and informal, institutional and non-institutional nodes of learning. (Loveless & Williamson, 2013, p. 53)

However, this new digitally enriched and connected learner engaged in social innovation networks is not yet liberated. The conditions in which learners can work together using effective pedagogies to meet the needs of their communities require ongoing questioning and dissent—particularly in instances where the culture of innovation is an institutionalised manifestation of cybernetic capitalism (see, e.g., Peters, 2015b). It appears not that there is an absence of ideas or that these ideas might be innovative, when conditions are closed, compartmentalised, individualised and prohibitive, but rather that these ontological/epistemological experiences/processes shape, limit, narrow and exploit thinking. For instance, a competitive test and reward system for assessment of student learning obstructs the flow and sharing of ideas and the nature of innovation. Through such obstructions students understand their autonomy as being an expression of consumer choices (Anderson, 1993). If the student is to be thought of as a producer, then this process of production is limited to the production of the self in the form of human capital (skills and knowledge); the exception being when tertiary students, mostly at the postgraduate level, publish materials that are then uploaded online. However, for the most part, the domain is a received domain where autonomy, as an expressive action of independent movement, is expressed in the form that is theoretically delimited to one of consumer choice, where the range of choice is *a priori*. The limits of the student's independent movement within this interpretation of the networked information economy are instrumentally delineated through the separation of the learning domain from the domain of paid employment according to the ontological distinction that separates the nonproprietary from the proprietary.

Technologies in the networked information economy have facilitated new social relations, a motif that might very quickly be assumed to mean that everything about We-Think may be thought to be positive, such that any historical problems that confronted the need for an explanation of the role the individual plays in innovation could be abandoned. It is very easy to stigmatize the problems of I-Think and the lone inventor and the heroic creator through a linguistic capacity to allude to the exhaustion of their function: Individuals no longer create alone and, in fact, they never have; this is the refrain, and yet we are still individuals who, on account of our diversity, think distinctive thoughts and distinctive interpretations of the same thought. For We-Think to be an effective description of a new form of collaborative coproduction in the networked information economy, the singularity of the individual innovative subject needs to be theorized. Furthermore, innovation itself must be critiqued as a concept for reason that the meaning of social innovation can change from theorist to theorist and according to how they understand the concept of innovation. When social innovation shares an epistemological foundation with social entrepreneurship, it would suppose that social innovation also shares an epistemological foundation with that of technological innovation, which is often that which provides the impetus for social innovation in the first place.

NOTES

1. See the declaration at http://www.capetowndeclaration.org/.
2. Lévy (1997) also differentiated between the industrial economy and the networked information economy by differentiating between the *cogito* and the *cogitamos* (p. 17).
3. Schumpeter's (1911/1934) own stipulation is that "we must never assume that the carrying out of a new combinations takes place by employing means of production which happens to be unused" (p. 67).
4. See also the notion of Cooperation Studies Curriculum and the list of resources at http://www.cooperationcommons.com/node/411, including papers by Howard Rheingold, who established the site. See also the list of papers on 'Collective Cognition' at http://vserver1.cscs.lsa.umich.edu/~crshalizi/notebooks/collective-cognition.html

REFERENCES

Anderson, E. (1993). *Value in ethics and economics.* London, UK: Harvard University Press.

Benkler, Y. (2006). *The wealth of networks: How social production transforms markets and freedom.* London, UK: Yale University Press.

Bollier, D. (2006). *When push comes to pull: The new economy and culture of networking technology.* A Report of the Fourteenth Annual Aspen Institute Roundtable on Information Technology. Washington, DC: The Aspen Institute. Retrieved from http://bollier.org/sites/default/files/aspen_reports/2005InfoTechText.pdf

Brown, L., Griffiths, R., & Rascoff, M. (2007). University publishing in a digital age. *The Journal of Electronic Publishing*, *10*(3). doi: http://dx.doi.org.ezproxy.aut.ac.nz/10.3998/3336451.0010.301

Chesbrough, H. (2003). *Open innovation: The new imperative for creating and profiting from technology.* Boston, MA: Harvard Business School Press.

Chesbrough, H. (2006). *Open business models: How to thrive in the new innovation landscape.* Boston, MA: Harvard Business School Press.

Chesbrough, H., Vanhaverbeke, W., & West, J. (Eds.). (2006). *Open innovation: Researching a new paradigm.* Oxford, UK: Oxford University Press.

Finholt, T. A. (2002). Collaboratories. *Annual Review of Information Science and Technology, 36*, 73–107.

Finholt, T. A., & Olson, G. M. (1997). From laboratories to collaboratories: A new organizational form for scientific collaboration. *Psychological Science, 8*(1), 28–36.

Foucault, M. (1983). "The Subject and Power." In M. Foucault. Beyond Structuralism and Hermeneutics, edited by H. Dreyfus and P. Rabinow, pp. 208-226. 2nd ed. Chicago: The University of Chicago Press.

Kant, I. (1959). *Foundations of the metaphysics of morals and what is enlightenment* (L. White Trans.). New York, NY: Liberal Arts Press.

Leadbeater, C. (2008). *We-Think: Mass innovation, not mass production.* London, UK: Profile Books.

Lévy, P. (1997). *Collective intelligence: Mankind's emerging world in cyberspace* (R. Bononno, Trans.). London, UK: Plenum Trade.

Loveless, A., & Williamson, B. (2013). *Learning identities in a digital age: Rethinking creativity, education and technology.* New York, NY: Routledge.

Materu, P. N. (2004). *Open source courseware: A baseline study.* Retrieved from http://siteresources.worldbank.org.ezproxy.aut.ac.nz/INTAFRREGTOPTEIA/Resources/open_source_courseware.pdf

McAfee, N. (2009). On democracy's epistemic value. *The Good Society, 18*, 41–47.

Michael A Peters (2012) *Education, Philosophy and Politics: Selected Works of Michael A. Peters*, New York: Routledge

Mill, V. D. (2002). Freedom of speech. *Stanford Encyclopedia of Philosophy.* Retrieved from http://plato.stanford.edu/entries/freedom-speech/

Momigliano, A. (2003). Freedom of speech in antiquity. *Dictionary of the History of Ideas.* Retrieved from http://etext.virginia.edu/cgi-local/DHI/dhi.cgi?id=dv2-31

Mulgan, G. (2013, November 14–15). *The study of social innovation: Theory, practice and progress.* Keynote presentation at the NESTA Social Frontiers Research Conference, Glasgow Caledonian University, London, UK. Retrieved from http://www.nesta.org.uk/event/social-frontiers

OECD. (2007). *Giving knowledge for free: The emergence of open educational resources.* Paris: OECD. Retrieved from http://www.oecd.org/edu/ceri/38654317.pdf

Page, S. (2007). *The difference: How the power of diversity creates better groups, firms, schools, and societies.* Princeton, NJ: Princeton University Press.

Peters, M. A. (2009). The history and emergent paradigm of open education. In M. A. Peters & R. G. Britez (Eds.), *Open education and education for openness* (pp. 3–16). Rotterdam, The Netherlands: Sense.

Peters, M. A. (2015a). Interview with Pierre A. Lévy, French philosopher of collective intelligence. *Open Review of Educational Research, 2*(1), 259–266. Retrieved from http://dx.doi.org/10.1080/23265507.2015.1084477

Peters, M. A. (2015b). The university in the epoch of digital reason: Fast knowledge in the circuits of cybernetic capitalism. *Analysis and Metaphysics, 14,* 7–27.

Schumpeter, J. (1934). *The theory of economic development: An inquiry into profits, capital, credit, interest, and the business cycle* (R. Opie, Trans.). Cambridge, MA: Harvard University Press. (Original work published 1911)

Unger, R. (2013, November 14–15). *Social frontiers.* Keynote presentation at the NESTA Social Frontiers Research Conference, Glasgow Caledonian University, London, UK. Retrieved from http://www.nesta.org.uk/event/social-frontiers

Von Hippel, E. (2005). *Democratizing innovation.* Cambridge, MA: The MIT Press. Retrieved from http://web.mit.edu/evhippel/www/democ1.htm

Weber, S. (2004). *The success of open source.* Cambridge, MA: Harvard University Press.

Editors

Michael A. Peters is Professor of Education at Waikato University, Emeritus Professor at the University of Illinois at Urbana-Champaign and Adjunct Professor in the School of Art, Royal Melbourne Institute of Technology (RMIT) and School of Foreign Studies, Guangzhou University. He is the executive editor of *Educational Philosophy and Theory* and editor of two international ejournals, *Policy Futures in Education* and *E-Learning and Digital Media*. His interests are in education, philosophy and social policy, and he has written over sixty books, including most recently *Education Philosophy and Politics: Selected Works of Michael A. Peters* (2011); *Education, Cognitive Capitalism and Digital Labour* (2011), with Ergin Bulut; *Neoliberalism and After? Education, Social Policy and the Crisis of Capitalism* (2011); *The Last Book of Postmodernism: Apocalyptic Thinking, Philosophy and Education in the Twenty-First Century* (2011); *Bakhtinian Pedagogy: Opportunities and Challenges for Research, Policy and Practice in Education Across the Globe* (2011), with Jayne White; *The Virtues of Openness: Education, Science and Scholarship in a Digital Age* (2011), with Peter Roberts; *Education in the Creative Economy* (2010), with D. Araya; the trilogy, *Creativity and the Global Knowledge Economy* (2009), *Global Creation: Space, Connection and Universities in the Age of the Knowledge Economy* (2010), *Imagination: Three Models of Imagination in the Age of the Knowledge Economy* (2010), all with Simon Marginson & Peter Murphy; *Subjectivity and Truth: Foucault, Education and the Culture of the Self* (2008) (The American Educational Studies Association Critics Book Award 2009), and *Building Knowledge Cultures:*

Education and Development in the Age of Knowledge Capitalism (2006), both with Tina Besley.

Markus Deimann is an Assistant Professor at the Fern Universität in Hagen (Germany) and has done extensive research within the topic of Open Education. He is Associate Editor of *Open Review of Educational Research* and a member of the editorial board for *E-Learning and Digital Media*. His interests are in education, philosophy and the digital transformation of society. He has been an advisor for political bodies in Germany in the area of (online) higher education.

CONTRIBUTORS

Robert Farrow is an interdisciplinary researcher and philosopher with the Institute of Educational Technology, The Open University (United Kingdom). He has worked on a range of research projects in the field of educational technology (including MOTILL (Mobile Technologies in Lifelong Learning), EU4ALL, OLnet and OER Research Hub). Most recently he worked with the Open Education Research Hub to conduct and promote high-quality research in open education.

Andrew Gibbons is an early childhood teacher educator and associate professor at the School of Education, Auckland University of Technology (New Zealand). His research focuses on the construction and experience of the early childhood teaching profession, drawing on the philosophy of early childhood education and the philosophy of technology. His book, *The Matrix Ate My Baby* (Sense), critiques the role of new media in early childhood education. In *Education, Ethics and Existence: Camus and the Human Condition* (Routledge, coauthored with Peter Roberts and Richard Heraud), he explores the contribution of Albert Camus for the critique of schooling. Gibbons is coeditor of the *Encyclopaedia of Educational Philosophy and Theory* and associate editor of *Educational Philosophy and Theory* and *Early Education*.

Richard Hall is professor of education and technology at De Montfort University (DMU), Leicester (United Kingdom). At DMU, he is head of enhancing learning through technology and leads the Education Futures Centre. Hall is a National Teaching Fellow and a cooperator at the Social Science Centre in Lincoln (United Kingdom).

Richard Heraud is in the process of completing a PhD at the University of Waikato (New Zealand). His research addresses the question of how the concept of innovation is understood in education. It has led him to examine questions related to the problem of understanding the formation of collective intelligence in education and how subjectivity is exercised in relation to the formation of new ideas in a collaborative dynamic, with a particular interest in the recent work of Pierre Lévy.

Theo Hug is professor of educational sciences at the University of Innsbruck (Austria) and coordinator of the Innsbruck Media Studies research forum. His areas of interest include media education and philosophy of education, mobile learning and microlearning, research methodology, theory of knowledge and philosophy of science.

Jeremy Knox is a lecturer on digital education with the University of Edinburgh (Scotland) and a core member of the Digital Cultures in Education research group. Research interests include critical posthumanism, new materialism and the implications of such thinking for education and educational research. He is currently working on a project titled "Artcasting," funded by the Arts & Humanities Research Council (United Kingdom), to develop mobile applications for museum and gallery evaluation; the SHEILA (Supporting Higher Education to Incorporate Learning Analytics) project, funded by Erasmus+, to develop learning analytics policy, and the The Learning Analytics Report Card (LARC) project to develop student-centered forms of data analysis for education. Knox designed and taught the E-learning and Digital Cultures MOOC (EDCMOOC) partnered with Coursera. He is the author of numerous publications in the field of digital education and a forthcoming book entitled *Posthumanism and the MOOC: Contaminating the Subject of Global Education* (Routledge).

Petra Missomelius is a research assistant in the Faculty of Education at Leopold-Franzens-University in Innsbruck (Austria) in the fields of media education and communication culture, and she is a member of the Innsbruck Media Studies research forum. Her current projects include "App to Apt," a study within the scope of a research project on personal analytics, self-image and self-care, as well as a habilitation treatise titled "Education in the Context of Post-Transformative Media Cultures."

Martin Oliver is professor of education and technology at the UCL Institute of Education (United Kingdom). His research explores issues of design, use and experience, with interests in roles, identities and curricula. He is a past president of the Association for Learning Technology, and he has edited the journals *Learning, Media & Identity* and *Research in Learning Technology*.

Robert Schuwer is professor of OER at Fontys University of Applied Sciences, School of ICT (Information and Communication Technologies) in Eindhoven (the Netherlands). Since 2006, the majority of his work discusses OER (Open Educational Resources) and open education. His experiences and research interests are in open policies, business models for OER and the implementation of OER-based processes on the institutional, cross-institutional and national levels.

Peter B. Sloep is full professor of technology enhanced learning (TEL) at the Welten Institute of The Open University (the Netherlands). He is honorary professor at the Caledonian Academy of Glasgow, Caledonian University (United Kingdom). His research encompasses such topics as networked learning (specifically but not exclusively for professionals), learning design, open educational resources, learning objects, standards for learning technologies, as well as knowledge sharing and creative collaboration in communities and networks. He has coauthored more than 200 peer-reviewed publications in scholarly journals and conference proceedings, and he has coauthored or edited three books. Dr. Sloep is a frequent speaker at national and international conferences. He frequently reviews papers for various journals and conferences in the TEL field.

David Small, BA (Hons), LLB, PhD, is a senior lecturer in education at the University of Canterbury in Christchurch, New Zealand. He is also a barrister of the High Court of New Zealand. His current research interests include racism and ethnicity, higher education, neoliberalism and globalization, and academic freedom and the surveillance state. Dr. Small is active in a range of social justice groups and academic associations, particularly in comparative and international education.

GLOBAL STUDIES IN EDUCATION

A.C. (Tina) Besley, Michael A. Peters,
Cameron McCarthy, Fazal Rizvi
General Editors

Global Studies in Education is a book series that addresses the implications of the powerful dynamics associated with globalization for re-conceptualizing educational theory, policy and practice. The general orientation of the series is interdisciplinary. It welcomes conceptual, empirical and critical studies that explore the dynamics of the rapidly changing global processes, connectivities and imagination, and how these are reshaping issues of knowledge creation and management and economic and political institutions, leading to new social identities and cultural formations associated with education.

We are particularly interested in manuscripts that offer: a) new theoretical, and methodological, approaches to the study of globalization and its impact on education; b) ethnographic case studies or textual/discourse based analyses that examine the cultural identity experiences of youth and educators inside and outside of educational institutions; c) studies of education policy processes that address the impact and operation of global agencies and networks; d) analyses of the nature and scope of transnational flows of capital, people and ideas and how these are affecting educational processes; e) studies of shifts in knowledge and media formations, and how these point to new conceptions of educational processes; f) exploration of global economic, social and educational inequalities and social movements promoting ethical renewal.

For additional information about this series or for the submission of manuscripts, please contact one of the series editors:

A.C. (Tina) Besley: t.besley@waikato.ac.nz
Cameron McCarthy: cmccart1@illinois.edu
Michael A. Peters: mpeters@waikato.ac.nz
Fazal Rizvi: frizvi@unimelb.edu.au

To order other books in this series, please contact our Customer Service Department:
  (800) 770-LANG (within the U.S.)
  (212) 647-7706 (outside the U.S.)
  (212) 647-7707 FAX

Or browse online by series:
  www.peterlang.com